Palm Pre™
Made Simple

Written for the
Palm® Pre™

Another in the
***Made Simple*™**
Guide Book Series

By
Martin Trautschold
Gary Mazo

Made Simple Learning is a CMT Publications, Inc. Company and is an independent source of training for the Palm Pre not affiliated with, nor endorsed by, Palm, Inc. of Sunnyvale, California, USA.

The Palm Pre™
Made Simple

This book is intended to help owners of the Palm Pre Series of Phones.

Please check out our electronic versions at
www.MadeSimpleLearning.com

Published by
CMT Publications, Inc.
25 Forest View Way
Ormond Beach, FL 32174

Copyright © 2009 by CMT Publications, Inc., Ormond Beach, Florida, USA

10-Digit ISBN: 1-4392-5524-5
13-Digit EAN: 9781439255247
Published Date: October 25, 2009

Published in the United States of America

10 9 8 7 6 5 4 3 2 1

Images
Palm Pre images courtesy of Palm, Inc.
(www.palm.com)
All other images are protected by copyrights of their respective owners.

Contact Us
Contact the authors at
info@MadeSimpleLearning.com
For Free Email Tips, Video Tutorials, and the Electronic Version ("E-book") in Adobe PDF format, please visit: www.MadeSimpleLearning.com

Brief Contents

Table of Contents

Check out our web site at www.MadeSimpleLearning.com

Chapter 9: Calendar 150

Chapter 10: Email 171

Contents

Check out our web site at www.MadeSimpleLearning.com

Authors & Acknowledgements

Martin Trautschold is the Founder and CEO of Made Simple Learning, a leading provider of Smartphone Training Videos and Books. Made Simple Learning originally developed training videos and books for the RIM BlackBerry family of smartphones, and is now excited to be expanding to the Palm® Pre™, Apple® iPhone™, iPod™ touch devices. Martin has been a successful entrepreneur in the smartphone training and software business for the past nine years. He has been helping to train thousands of BlackBerry users with hundreds of short, to-the-point, video tutorials and has also co-authored eleven "Made Simple" guide books. Gary Mazo has been Martin's co-author on all the most recent books. Martin and Gary teamed up with Kevin Michaluk, founder of CrackBerry.com to write a part-serious, part-funny, but wholly entertaining guide to BlackBerry addiction called: "CrackBerry: True Tales of BlackBerry Use and Abuse."

Martin began his entrepreneurial life with a wireless software company which he co-founded with his brother-in-law, Ned Johnson. Together, they spent 3 years growing it and then sold it. The company's flagship product "Handheld Contact" is still being developed, marketed and sold by the new owners. Martin also has 15 years experience managing complex technology and business projects for consulting, technology and energy firms in the US and Japan. He holds a Bachelor of Science in Engineering Degree from Princeton University and an MBA from the Kellogg School at Northwestern University. In his "free time" he enjoys spending time with his wife, Julie, and three children. Occasionally, he tries to sneak a few hours to row on the Halifax River with his daughter, Olivia, or ride his bicycle with friends in Ormond Beach, Florida. Martin can be reached at martin@madesimplelearning.com.

> I would like to thank my co-author Gary Mazo for his tireless effort in helping to make this book a success. This book is much more comprehensive due to his efforts. Special thanks goes out to all the Made Simple Learning customers who have asked great questions and shared their tips, many of which are in this book! I would also like to thank my wife, Julie and my daughters for their support over the many months of writing, re-writing and editing.
>
> -- Martin Trautschold

 **Gary Mazo** is a writer, a College Professor, a gadget nut and an ordained rabbi. Gary joined Made Simple Learning in 2007 and has co-authored the last eight books in the Made Simple Learning Series. He serves as VP of the company as well. Along with Martin and Kevin Michaluk from CrackBerry.com, Gary co-wrote "CrackBerry: True Tales of BlackBerry Use and Abuse" - a book about BlackBerry addiction and how to get a grip on one's BlackBerry use.

Gary also teaches at the University of Phoenix – teaching Writing, Philosophy, Technical Writing and more. Gary is a regular contributor to CrackBerry.com – writing product reviews and adding Editorial Content. Gary has also been the Director of Kollel of Cape Cod – a cutting edge Jewish Educational institution/Congregation in Marstons Mills, Massachusetts. He holds a BA in Anthropology from Brandeis University. Gary earned his M.A.H.L (Masters in Hebrew Letters) as well as ordination as Rabbi from the Hebrew Union College-Jewish Institute of Religion in Cincinnati, Ohio. He has served congregations in Dayton, Ohio, Cherry Hill, New Jersey and Hyannis, Massachusetts.

His first book, entitled "And the Flames Did Not Consume us" achieved critical acclaim and was published by Rising Star Press in 2000.

Gary is married to Gloria Schwartz Mazo and between them, they have six children. Gary can be reached at: gary@madesimplelearning.com.

This book is only possible due to the support of several individuals in my life. First, I would like to thank Martin Trautschold for giving me the opportunity to join him in this project. Next, I want to thank my wife, Gloria and our kids; Ari, Dan, Sara, Bill, Elise and Jonah – without whom I would not have the support to pursue projects like this one.

A very special 'thank you' to Dieter Bohn, Editor in Chief of Smartphone Experts, for lending his expertise by writing the "Homebrew Apps" Chapter, which starts on page 341.

-- Gary Mazo

Other Made Simple Learning Products

Formerly BlackBerry Made Simple

Books & Training Center DVD-ROMs

iPod touch® *Made Simple*
iPhone® 3G *Made Simple*
CrackBerry: True Tales of BlackBerry® Use and Abuse
BlackBerry Tour™ 9600 *Made Simple*
BlackBerry Bold™ 9000 *Made Simple*
BlackBerry Curve™ 8900 *Made Simple*
BlackBerry Curve™ 8350i *Made Simple*
BlackBerry Pearl™ 'Flip' 8200 *Made Simple*
BlackBerry Pearl *Made Simple* for 8100 Series
 BlackBerry smartphones
BlackBerry Curve 8300/8800 Series *Made Simple*
BlackBerry *Made Simple*™ for Full Keyboard BlackBerry
 smartphones (87xx, 77xx, 75xx, 72xx, 6xxx Series)
BlackBerry *Made Simple*™ for 7100 Series BlackBerry
 smartphones (7100, 7130, 71xx Series)

Videos Now™

Video Training Viewed On Your Computer

We are building out our full library of more than
50 video training clips designed specifically for
your Palm Pre.

Videos To Go™
Video Training You Watch on your Smartphone

Video training you download watch right on your
Palm Pre.

Visit our site to check out the latest Palm Pre
video tutorials: www.madesimplelearning.com

Quick Reference Guide

Getting Started

The items below will help you get up and running with your Palm Pre.

To Do This...	Use This...	Where to Learn More
Turn on or off the Palm Pre	Power / Sleep Key	Press and hold this key on the top right edge. Page 37
Start the Phone, Place a Call	Phone Icon	Page 101
Turn off the Ringer	Ringer / Mute Switch	Slide this key to Mute / Un-Mute switch on the top. Page 38
Check Voicemail	Voicemail Icon	Page 113
Use the Camera	Camera App	Page 224
Send a Message	Messaging App	Page 195
Buy Music	Amazon MP3 App	Page 266

To Do This...	Use This...	Where to Learn More
Return to Home Screen	**"Center" Button**	Page 38
Unlock Your Phone	**Drag to Unlock**	Page 40
Start Listening to Music	**Music App**	Page 253
Sync Music, Videos and Pictures with your Computer	**iTunes (for Windows™) and Apple™ Mac™)**	Page 85
Start Watching Videos	**Videos**	Page 273
Surf the Web	**Web Browser**	Page 206
Read "Office" Documents	**Doc View**	Page 190

Stay Organized

Use these things to stay in organized with your Palm Pre.

To Do This...	Use This...	Where to Learn More
Manage Your Contact Names & Numbers	**Address Book**	Page 133
Manage your Calendar	**Calendar**	Page 150
Take notes, store your grocery list and more!	**Memos**	Page 298
Look at, Manage, Organize your Pictures	**Photos**	Page 234
View & Send Email	**Mail**	Page 175
Calculate your MPG, a meal tip, and convert units!	**Calculator**	Page 309
Set a wakeup alarm, use a countdown timer or stopwatch	**Date and Time**	Page 63
Find just about Anything, get Directions	**Google Maps**	Page 288

Be Entertained

Use these things to have fun with your Palm Pre!

To Do This...	Use This...	Where to Learn More
Quickly get to all your Music!	**Music**	Page 253
Look at, Zoom in and Organize your Pictures	**Photos**	Page 234
Watch Movies and Music Videos	**Videos**	Page 273
Browse and Download Apps right to your Palm Pre	**App Catalog**	Page 320

Learning Your Palm Pre:
The Screen, Buttons, Switches and Ports

Name of your current Wireless network

TIP: Inside icons, you tap here or swipe down to see menus.

Headphone Jack

Status Bar

Mute Switch
When you see orange, it is Muted

Wake/Sleep – On/Off Button
Tap to sleep or wake up, press & hold to power on or off.

Battery (shows charging)

Bluetooth	Wi-Fi	Cellular
When visible	**Signal** When White	**Signal** 1-5 bars

Volume Up & Down Keys

USB Charging/Sync Port
Connect to computer to Charge, Sync Music, Videos and more.

Quick Launch Bar
These icons are always visible. TIP: You can customize this with your own "Top 4 Icons."

Launcher Icon
Touch to see all Icons

Notification Bar & Dashboard Area
Tap a notification to see more or operate the on-screen dashboard control.

Center Button
Show/Hide Cards for Multi-Tasking. Tap once to reduce an application to its "Card View"

Orange or "ALT" Key
Use to type numbers, symbols on upper part of each key and used in many shortcut key combinations.

Shift Key
Use to upper case and use to start selection for Copy/Paste.

"@" and "."
Handy to use when typing email or web addresses.

Symbol Key
Use to type symbols not shown on keyboard.

Enter Key
Confirm a selection, enter text.

Learning When You are Connected to a Network (Top Status Bar)

It is helpful to understand the symbols and letters in the upper portion of the screen in the black Status Bar. Knowing how to read these can help you save time when wondering if you can use email, browse the web or make phone calls.

Status Symbols	Bluetooth	Wi-Fi	Cell Network	Battery
✱ 📶 🔋	On, but not connected	On and Connected	Connected (Low Speed, Med. Signal)	Charging (half full)
📶 Ev 🔋	Off	On, not connected	Connected (High Speed, Strong signal)	Charging (almost full)
Ev 🔋	Off	Off	Connected (Low Speed)	Charging (fully charged)
⊕ 📶 🔋	On, in process of connecting	On and connected	Connected (Low Speed, Weak signal)	Charging (fully charged)
✱ 📶 🔋	On, connected to one or more devices.	On and connected	Connected (Low Speed, Weak signal)	Charging (fully charged)
✈ 🔋 (Airplane Mode)	Off	Off	Off	Charging

Airplane Mode – How to turn it on or off

When you are boarding a plane, you will want to enable "Airplane Mode." Simply swipe your hand down or tap in the upper right corner (where all the wireless status indicators are located) and select "Turn On Airplane Mode" from the menu.

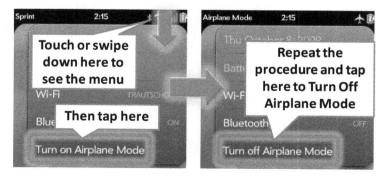

Using the Launcher and Starting Icons

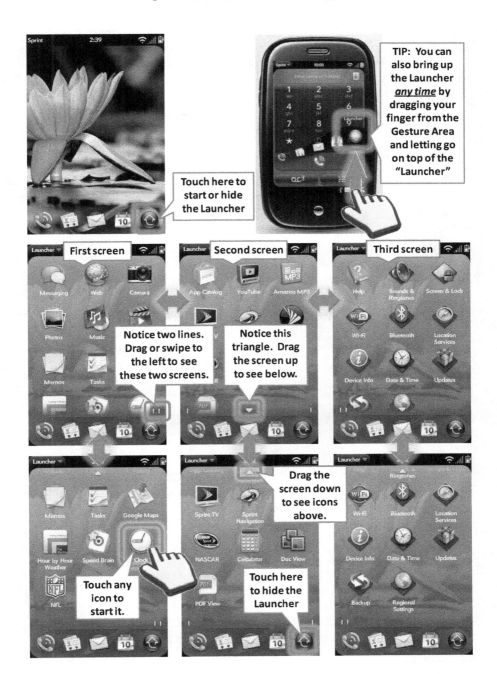

TIP: You can also bring up the Launcher *any time* by dragging your finger from the Gesture Area and letting go on top of the "Launcher"

Touch here to start or hide the Launcher

First screen — Notice two lines. Drag or swipe to the left to see these two screens.

Second screen — Notice this triangle. Drag the screen up to see below.

Third screen

Drag the screen down to see icons above.

Touch any icon to start it.

Touch here to hide the Launcher

Your Palm Pre Touch Screen

The Palm Pre™ has combined an amazingly sensitive and intuitive touch screen with a slide out keyboard. Palm®, renown for making Personal Digital Assistants ("PDAs"), has come up with an excellent touch screen. Palm has also added a slide out Keyboard for Typing – so the screen is always available in its entirety and you never have to "type on glass."

You can pretty much do anything on your Palm Pre™ by using a combination of:

- Touch screen 'gestures;'
- Touching any icon or soft key on the screen;
- Using the "Center Button" at the bottom; and,
- Sliding out the Keyboard when you need to type.

Like many of the newer touch screen phones, the Pre relies on using "Gestures" to help you move through screens, launch application and navigate through Apps. Once the "Setup" process is complete, the Pre will show you short explanations of some of the main "Gestures" you can perform.

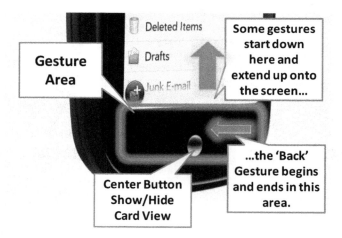

Some "Gestures" can be performed in the main screen and this will be explained as we move on. There is an area below the screen and extending to both sides of the "Center Button" which is known as the "Gesture Area."

The best are for performing many of the gestures is the "Gesture Area" which is the area between the bottom of the screen and the top of the "Center Button."

Key Gestures, Buttons and Icons:

- **Touch** – To start an Icon, confirm a selection, select a menu item, or select an answer simply touch the screen.
- **Back - Short Swipe Left -** To back out of something (icon, selection, menu), use a short quick "right to left" swipe inside the Gesture Area.
- **Center Button** – To minimize an icon you are in to a Card, or maximize the selected (center most) card to fill the screen, tap the Center Button.
- **Long Swipe Left or Right** – To switch between open icons, perform a long swipe left or right in the Gesture Area. This must be enabled in Screen & Lock (Advanced Gestures) – see page 252.
- **Half-Way Up** – **"Ride the Wave"** – To start any icons in the Quick Launch Bar (even if you cannot see it), drag your finger from the Gesture Area half way up the screen. The Quick Launch Bar will appear as a 'wave.' Then slide your finger back/forth to select the icon under your finger – see page 23.
- **Launcher - Long Up** – Start in the Gesture Area and swipe all the way to the top of the phone to bring up or hide the Launcher -- see page 23.
- **Launcher – Icon** – Touch the Launcher Icon ![icon] in the bottom left corner to show/hide the Launcher – which shows all your icons on your phone.
- **Throw Away Cards -** To close the Card (icon) in the center of the screen, swipe it up and off the top of the phone. (See page 26)
- **Touch and Scroll (Swipe)** – To move in a direction (screens, pictures, menu items, lists) simply swipe left, right, up or down. You can hold your finger on the screen and swipe as slowly or quickly as you like.
- **Flick** – To quickly move up or down in an email, web page, pictures or list, quickly "Flick" up and down the screen.
- **Throw Away Notifications** – To close a notification or alert message you see at the bottom of the screen drag or swipe it left or right (off the screen.)
- **Swipe from Top Corner for Menus** – Swipe from either top corner to bring up menus.
- **Double Tap** – **Zoom in / Zoom out** shortcut for a web page or picture. Double-tap once to zoom In and then again to zoom out.
- **Open Pinch / Close Pinch** – **Zoom In / Zoom Out**. When viewing a picture or web page, pinch your thumb and forefinger together then touch the screen and slide the fingers apart to zoom in. Use the opposite to zoom out.

Starting Apps, Card View and Multi-Tasking

Touch any icon to start the App. Press the Center Button to minimize it to Card View. Flick left/right between cards. Flick up to close or 'throw away' a card. TIP: Tap anywhere off the cards to switch between "Large" and "Small" Card Views. In "Small" Card View, drag cards up and left or right to re-arrange the order of the cards.

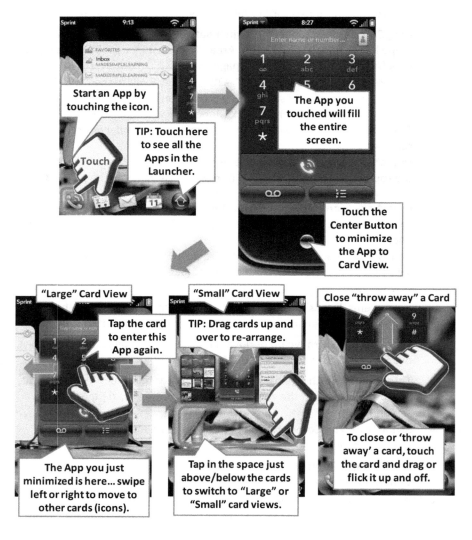

Ride the Wave to Start Quick Launch Apps

Starting inside the Gesture Area, drag your finger half way up the screen and keep your finger on the screen. You will see that the four Apps set for the "Quick Launch Bar" will then move up in a "Wave."

You can move your finger left or right through the "Wave" – let go when your finger is on the correct App to start it up.

If you wanted to start the Calendar App, move your finger so the calendar is on the top of the wave the Calendar name is showing and let go.

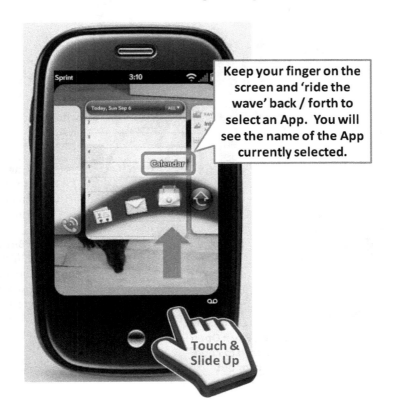

Keep your finger on the screen and 'ride the wave' back / forth to select an App. You will see the name of the App currently selected.

Touch & Slide Up

Basic Touch Gestures

You can do almost everything on your Pre with a few basic gestures, the Center Button and Launcher icon.

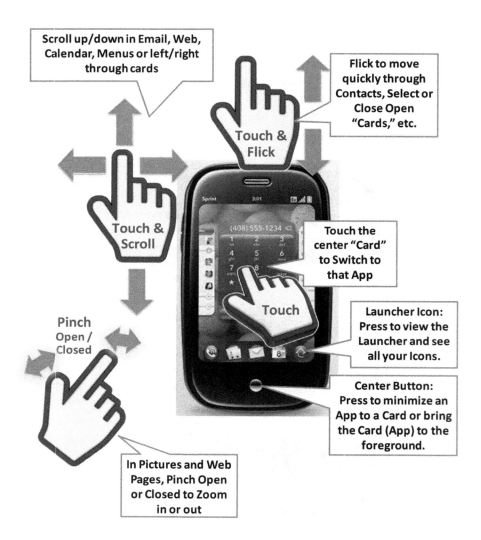

Scroll up/down in Email, Web, Calendar, Menus or left/right through cards

Flick to move quickly through Contacts, Select or Close Open "Cards," etc.

Touch & Flick

Touch & Scroll

Touch the center "Card" to Switch to that App

Pinch Open / Closed

Touch

Launcher Icon: Press to view the Launcher and see all your Icons.

Center Button: Press to minimize an App to a Card or bring the Card (App) to the foreground.

In Pictures and Web Pages, Pinch Open or Closed to Zoom in or out

Swipe Gesture

Swiping left or right is a great way to move between photos in your Photos album, move around a web page or move between Cards on the home screen. To swipe, you place your finger on the screen and drag it left or right while holding it on the screen. TIP: You can slow down or stop any time or swipe as quickly as you like.

Showing, Hiding and Navigating Menus

You will soon notice that most icons have a menu in the upper left corner that you access by tapping it with your finger or quickly swiping down in the same area. To hide this menu, tap your finger anywhere on the screen away from the menu. To go back one level or close the menu, use the "BACK" gesture – a quick left to right motion in the Gesture Area.

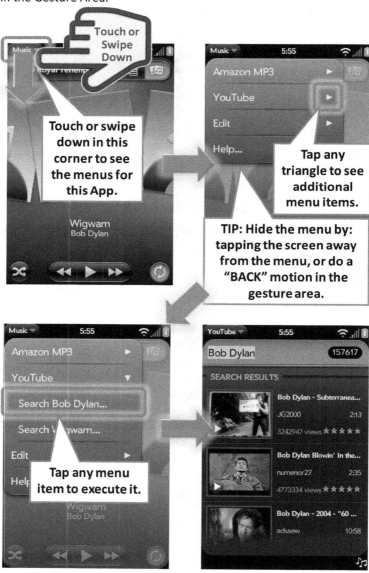

Settings / Preferences On Your Pre

Unlike some other Smartphones, the Pre does not have a single **"Settings"** or **"Options"** icon. You will find a few separate icons for setting things usually located on the third launcher screen like **"Sounds & Ringtones,"** **"Screen & Lock,"** **"Wi-Fi,"** **"Bluetooth."**   However, you will find that most icons have of their own settings, called **"Preferences"** or **"Preferences & Accounts"** inside their icon menus.

In order to setup things like Email, Contacts and Calendar wireless synchronization, you will need to go into the **"Preferences & Accounts"** section of these icons. Once you know where to look for these types of settings, you will be able to setup, configure, and customize pretty much anything on your phone.

Playing Songs - Media Controls

When playing music, you can do just about anything you need with the controls at the bottom and top of the screen. Tap the bar at the top to switch between "Song View" and "Album/Playlist View." You can start new songs by tapping them in Album/Playlist View. Touch and drag left or right in "Song View" to change songs. The fast-forward and rewind icons at the bottom do double-duty: Tap once to advance or go back a song. Press and hold to fast-forward or rewind inside the song.

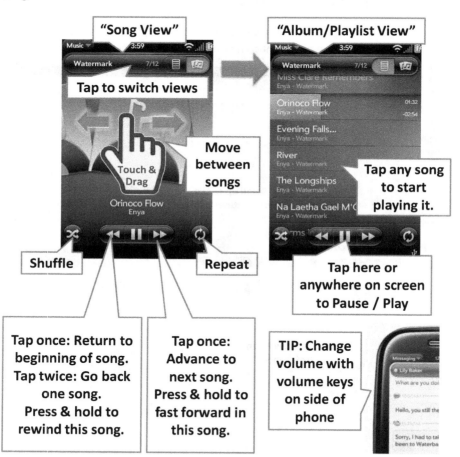

Playing Videos – Media Controls

As of publication, the Pre played all videos in horizontal or landscape mode. This makes the controls appear along the bottom of the screen as you hold the Pre on its side, or along the left side if you hold the Pre vertically.

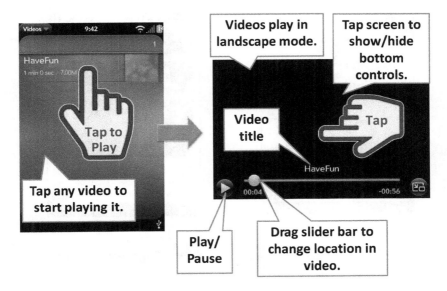

Videos play in landscape mode.

Tap screen to show/hide bottom controls.

Video title

Tap

Tap to Play

Tap any video to start playing it.

Play/ Pause

Drag slider bar to change location in video.

Copy & Paste – The Basics

First, select the text...

...Then, Cut / Copy and Paste.

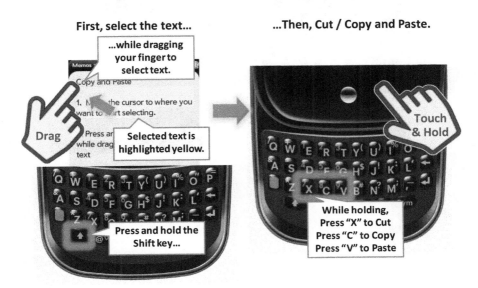

...while dragging your finger to select text.

Drag

Selected text is highlighted yellow.

Press and hold the Shift key...

Touch & Hold

While holding, Press "X" to Cut Press "C" to Copy Press "V" to Paste

Double Tap to Quickly Zoom In or Out

This works on Web Pages, Email Messages, and Pictures.

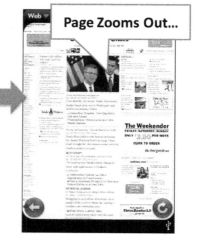

"Pinch" Open or Closed to Gradually Zoom Out or In

This Gesture works on Web Pages, Email Messages, PDF View, and Photos.

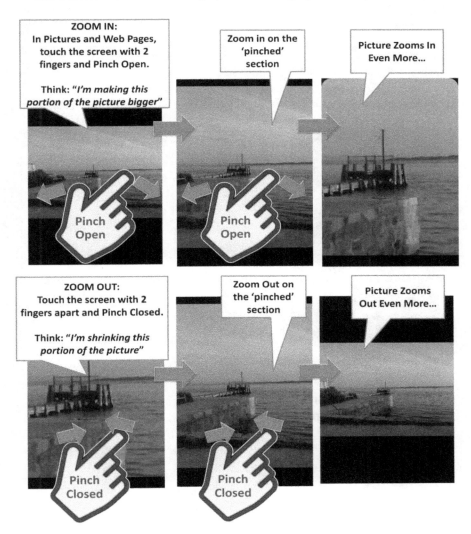

ZOOM IN:
In Pictures and Web Pages, touch the screen with 2 fingers and Pinch Open.

Think: *"I'm making this portion of the picture bigger"*

Zoom in on the 'pinched' section

Picture Zooms In Even More...

Pinch Open

Pinch Open

ZOOM OUT:
Touch the screen with 2 fingers apart and Pinch Closed.

Think: *"I'm shrinking this portion of the picture"*

Zoom Out on the 'pinched' section

Picture Zooms Out Even More...

Pinch Closed

Pinch Closed

Touch and Hold and "Throw/Slide" to Close or Delete

This is one of the fun features of the Palm Pre. When you are in **"Card View,"** just **"Touch and Hold"** a card and **"Throw"** the card upwards and off the top of the phone to close that App. It can be quite fun – akin to throwing papers off the top of your desk – when you don't have to pick them up!

If you have an email or other "Notification" at the bottom of the screen, just **"Touch and Slide"** the message to either side to cancel it.

If you have an Email in your list just **"Touch and Slide"** it to the right to "Delete."

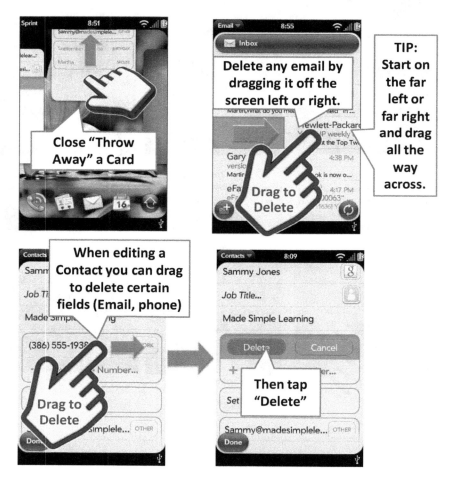

How to Correctly Disconnect the USB cable from your Computer

If you have been connecting your Pre to your computer to transfer files back and forth in "USB Drive" mode you may have seen the error message on your Pre that "Some data was damaged." This happens if you select "Safely Remove" instead of "Eject." On a Windows computer, open up Explorer (Start menu > Computer), locate the PALM PRE drive and right-click, select "Eject." On an Apple Mac, simply drag the PALM PRE drive image to the trash can to "Eject it" or "right click" and select "Eject."

How do you know when it is successfully ejected?

The Pre screen goes out of USB Drive mode back to the normal screen.

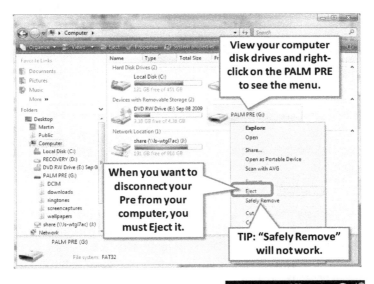

View your computer disk drives and right-click on the PALM PRE to see the menu.

When you want to disconnect your Pre from your computer, you must Eject it.

TIP: "Safely Remove" will not work.

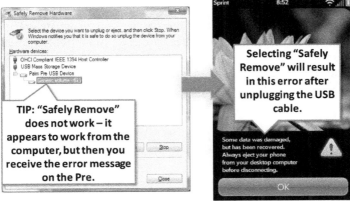

TIP: "Safely Remove" does not work – it appears to work from the computer, but then you receive the error message on the Pre.

Selecting "Safely Remove" will result in this error after unplugging the USB cable.

Some data was damaged, but has been recovered. Always eject your phone from your desktop computer before disconnecting.

OK

Introduction

Congratulations on your Palm Pre!

In your hands is perhaps the most original Smartphones with Personal Media Player available today – the Palm Pre.

> The "Original" Palm Pilot™ was a breakthrough device in Personal Information Management. The "Treo" series added the functionality of Phone and Email to that.

> The Pre takes thing to a whole new level with the brand new webOS™ Software, Synergy Syncing technology, and intuitive touch screen.

Things this powerful are not always easy to grasp – at first

> You will soon realize that your Palm Pre is a very powerful device. There are, however, many secrets "locked" inside that we help you "unlock" throughout this book.

> Anyone new to a touch screen on a phone may not see Palm's "intuitive" design at first glance. This new touch screen might even be a little daunting – you want your Palm Pre to do what your old phone did – in just the same way. Your Pre has both a physical keyboard and a capacitive Touch Screen – so it can do much more.

> Take your time – this book can help you on your way to learning how to best use and work with your new Palm Pre. Think back to what you felt like when you first tried to use a Windows™ or Mac™ computer -- It took a little while to get familiar with how to do things. It's the same with the Palm Pre. Use this book to help you get up to speed and learn all the best tips and tricks more quickly.

Chapter 1:
The Basics

Before you do anything with your new Palm Pre, please take a few minutes to check out our "**Quick Reference Guide**" pages earlier in this book. They are meant to help you get up and running quickly.

Easy Cross Reference- Icons and What they Do – Page 15

Learn the screen, buttons and more - Page 37

Learn the touch screen 'gestures' – Page 22

Getting Your Pre Setup and Understanding Synergy™ - Page 53.

Powering On and Off and Sleep Mode

To Power On your Palm Pre, press and hold the power key on the top right edge of the Palm Pre for a few seconds. If your phone is completely off, you will need to hold the power button for about 3 seconds to have the phone power on.

Press & Hold to Power On or Off. Tap to Sleep/Wake.

The Power Button on the upper right edge doubles as the Sleep / Wake Up Button.

A short press of this button to put your Palm Pre into "Sleep" mode or to "Wake" it up when it is 'sleeping.' Opening the Keyboard or tapping the Center Button will also wake up the phone.

Depending on your time-out setting (see page 41), your Palm Pre will usually go into "Sleep Mode" by itself in 1-5 minutes. The advantage of **"Sleep Mode"** is that when you want to use your Palm Pre again, just a quick tap of the **"On/Off"** button will bring your Palm Pre back awake. This convenience comes at the price of battery life.

If you want to maximize your
battery life or if you know you
won't be using your Palm Pre for
quite some time - say when you
go to sleep - you might want to
turn it off completely. The way
to do this is to press and hold the
Power Button. You then have
the option to **"Turn off,"** go into
"Airplane Mode" (which turns
off your radio so you can safely
use your Pre on board an
aircraft) or **"Cancel."**

**TIP: There is a quicker way to
get to Airplane Mode, see page
20.**

The "Center" Button

The "Center" button is useful on your Pre™
for a few reasons. Most likely, you will use
this button to switch between "Maximizing"
a Card into an active App or "Minimizing"
an App to become a "Card" on the screen.

The Mute / Ringer Off and Volume Keys

MUTE / RINGER OFF KEY
Handy when going into that
movie, meal or meeting... this
switch will turn off the ringer on
the Palm Pre and can be set it to
vibrate when calls or messages
come in by sliding it to the right.
You know you have turned
MUTE on when you feel a brief
vibration and see a bell with a
line through it on the screen.
Also, you will see that an orange

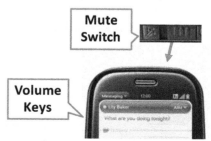

You will see this on the screen when
you switch the MUTE "ON."

dot (or orange area) is visible
next to the switch.

VOLUME KEYS
Located on the upper left hand side of the Palm Pre are simple Volume
up/volume down keys.

Your Launcher – Where you See and Start Your Apps

When you first look at your Pre screen, you are likely looking at the Home
Screen which shows you just the bottom dock and the main wallpaper
image. In order to see and start all your Icons, you will need to get into the
"**Launcher**." See page 21 for a full description of how to get into the
Launcher, navigate around and start Apps.

TIP: How to open several apps faster
You can open several apps at virtually the same time by tapping the icon
from the launcher or Quick Launch Bar then immediately pressing the
Center Button to turn the launching icon into a card. Use the "Ride the
Wave" trick (see page 21) to bring up the Quick Launch Bar to start
another icon or start the launcher and choose another icon to start.
Minimize that to a "Card" and repeat.

Quick Launch Bar - Use for your Favorite Apps

Another way to start your favorite icons is to touch them in the Quick
Launch Bar. You will see five icons "locked" in the "Quick Launch Bar"
while the rest of the icons can move back and forth in the Launcher pages
above this Quick Launch Bar. Learn how to move your favorite icons into
the Quick Launch Bar in our "Moving Icons" section on page 242.

Drag up to Unlock

When you first power on your Palm Pre, you may see the "Lock" icon. As soon as

you touch the "lock" icon [ ] you will see the words "drag up to unlock." You will see an "arc" on the screen - gently "Slide" the lock icon in any direction outside of the marked "arc" to unlock the screen.

Once you do that, you will see your Home Screen.

TIP: You can also open the keyboard to unlock your phone.

How to Secure your Phone with a PIN or Password

Many of us have important or sensitive information stored on our phones these days. If you want to be able to secure that information on your Pre, see page 250 for details about how to enable PIN or Password security.

Connecting Your Pre to Your Computer with the USB Cable

You will need to connect your Pre to your computer to charge it, sync your media, use it as a USB Drive (external disk drive or 'mass storage device'). The great thing about the Pre is that you can change the way it is connected without disconnecting the USB cable.

When You Connect the Pre to the Computer

Every time you connect your Pre to your computer, you will see three options pop up on the bottom of the screen:

Media Sync – This allows you to easily transfer media to your Pre using software such as iTunes™ or doubleTwist™. (See page 73

for more on Media Transfer). Note: You cannot make or receive calls or use text messaging in Media Sync mode.

USB Drive – This allows your Pre to look like another 'Removable Disk' drive on your computer. You may see it show up as "G:," "F:" or some other letter on your Windows computer, or see it pop up as a disk icon on your Mac desktop. This mode allows you to easily drag and drop files between the Pre and your computer. (See page 79 for more on transferring files and media using USB mode.)

Just Charge – Like it sounds, this mode will just charge your Pre and allow you to use it normally.

How do you change modes on the Pre screen after the USB cable is connected?

From "Just Charge" mode, simply tap the bottom of the screen – the USB icon to bring up the menu of three options. Select the different mode.

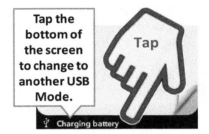

From "**Media Sync**" or "**USB Drive**" modes, you will first need to "**Eject**" the "**PALM PRE**" disk from your computer. This will get you into "**Just Charge**" mode, then follow the instructions above to select a different mode. (See how to do this on page 35.)

To Adjust "Auto Lock" or Sleep Mode Time Out

After you have your Palm Pre for just a little while, you will notice that it will "Auto Lock" and go into "Sleep Mode" with the screen blank after a short amount of time. You can change this time or even disable this feature altogether inside the "**Screen and Lock**" Icon.

Open your **Launcher** (see page 21), slide left or right until you see the "**Screen and Lock**" icon, then touch it. (It is usually on the third page of icons to the right.)

You will notice that there are a few other settings inside this icon, we show you how to use these in other sections in this book.

Adjust Brightness
– see page 44
Change Wallpaper
– see page 248
Advanced Gestures
– see page 252
Secure Unlock (Password/PIN)
– see page 250.

In this icon, you can decide if you want to be able to see "Notifications" when the screen is locked by just moving the "Show when locked" button to "On" or "Off."

The default setting is that the Palm Pre locks after one minute of sitting idle (to save battery life.) You can change this to 30 seconds or 2, or 3 minutes.

Just touch the desired setting to select it - you know it's selected when you see the checkmark next to it (like 2 minutes in the image).

BATTERY LIFE TIP:
Setting the Auto-Lock shorter (e.g. 30 seconds) will help you save battery life, but you may increase your frustration with the screen going blank too often.

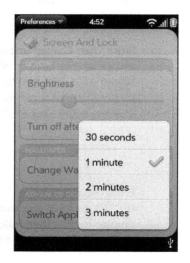

Adjusting the Date and Time

Usually, the date and time are adjusted automatically using the wireless phone network or when you connect your Palm Pre to your computer (which we cover in the next chapter). Here we will show you how to manually adjust your date and time.

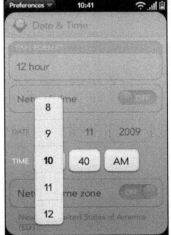

Touch the "**Date and Time**" icon from the Launcher. To set your time manually, you need to turn "OFF" "**Network time**" and "**Network time Zone**." Touch the switches to change them from "ON" to "OFF."

After turning "**Network Time**" to "OFF," you can then manually change the time.

When you turn "Network Time Zone" off, you can set any time zone you like.

Why might you want to turn off the Network Time Zone?
-   If you are travelling from one time zone to another, but want to keep your phone's time zone as your home time zone. (Could help you when scheduling meetings in your home time zone.)

12 hour vs. 24 Hour Time
If you prefer to see 09:30 and 14:30 instead of 9:30 AM and 2:30 PM, then you will want to set the Time Format from **12 hour** to **24 hour**.

Adjusting the Brightness

From your Home screen, touch the **"Screen and Lock"** icon. The **"Brightness"** tab is at the top of the screen. Touch the Brightness tab and then move the slider control to adjust the brightness.

Note: Your Palm Pre has an "Auto-Brightness" control that is not user adjustable.

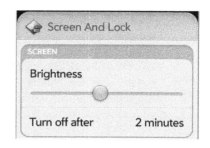

BATTERY LIFE TIP:
Setting the brightness lower will help you save battery life. A little less than 1/2 way across seems to work fine.

Typing and Keyboard Basics

As you begin to use your Palm Pre, one of the things you will need to get used to is typing on the slide-out keyboard.

TIP: To type any of the numbers or symbols on the upper part of each key, tap the Orange key once.

TIP: Make sure to remember the "@" and "." Keys when typing email addresses and web addresses, they can save you a lot of time.

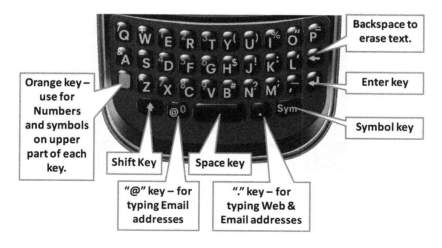

Typing with Two Thumbs

We recommend that you type with two thumbs instead of one finger. After you get the hang of it, you will be at least twice as fast as the single finger hunt-and-peck mode.

Typing Symbols Not on the Keyboard

Simply press the "Sym" key to type symbols you do not see on the keyboard. Remember that you can swipe down to see up to four additional pages of symbols. All current symbols are shown below. Tap any symbol to place it in the text you are typing.

TIP: Press and hold the Sym Key, then press a letter key to see only symbols related to that letter. For example if you wanted to just see all the accents for the letter "U", press and hold the Sym key then press the letter "U" key.

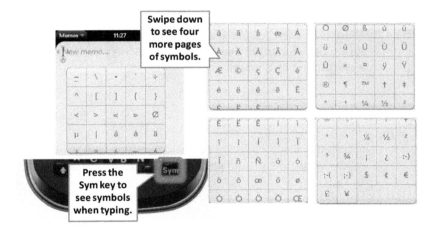

Typing: Num Lock / Upper Symbols on Keys (Orange Key) Lock

When you want to type several numbers in a row, or you want to only type the symbols on the top of the keys like "/" "&" "$" and more, tap the Orange key twice. NOTE: Tapping the Orange Key once will show you a blue circle under the cursor, meaning that only the next character typed will altered.

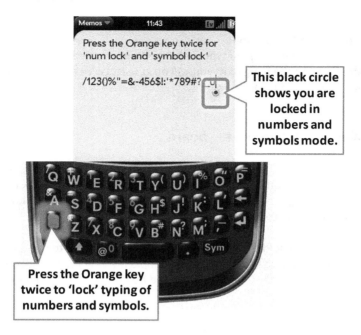

Notice that when you are in a phone number field (e.g. in Contacts or in the Phone), you do not need to press the Orange key to dial numbers, just press the keys by themselves.

Caps and Caps Lock (Upper Case)

If you tap the Shift key once, you will see a little blue arrow in a circle under the cursor – this shows that the next letter will be upper case.

Tap the Shift key twice to turn on 'Caps Lock' – you will see a Black arrow in the circle under the cursor showing you are in 'Caps Lock' mode. Tap the Shift key again to unlock Caps mode.

Positioning the Cursor for Editing Text

Say you saw a spelling or other mistake after typing an entire paragraph.
So you need to move the cursor back up to near the beginning of the page.

Simply tap your finger where you want to move the cursor. If you don't
get it exactly where you want to go, then try again.
TIP: Hold down the "Orange" button and then Drag on the screen to move
the cursor to a precise position.

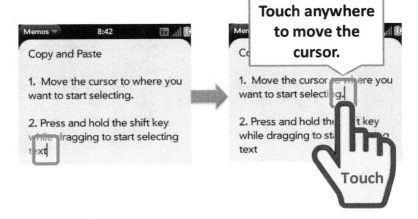

Copy and Paste with Your Pre

A great way to save time as well as increase your accuracy, is to use the built-in copy/paste functionality. You can even copy and paste text and images from the web and email. (See page 216).

NOTE: These steps for selecting text only work if you are actually typing and editing text. If you are reading text (email message or web page) then see page 216 for instructions on how to select and copy text and pictures.

Before you start to select text to cut or copy, you need to tap the screen to position the cursor at the beginning or end of the text block.

Then press and hold the SHIFT key while dragging your finger to select the text – you will notice the text be highlighted with yellow.

TIP: A quick way to "Select All" text is to touch the Gesture Area and press the letter "A" on the keyboard.

Once you have selected the text, you have several ways to "Cut" or "Copy" the text.

One way is to tap the upper left corner (or swipe down) to bring up the Menu and select "Cut or Copy".

TIP: You know you have cut or copied correctly when you see a "Selection Cut" or "Selection Copied" message at the bottom of your screen.

Another way is to use the Gesture + Keyboard Shortcuts. You can see each short cut on the menu. For example "Cut" is Touch and Hold the Gesture Area + press the "X" key.

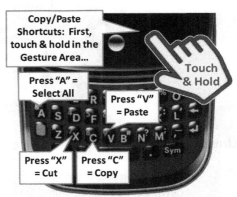

After you have Cut or Copied the text, then navigate to where you want to paste it.

If you want to paste it into another application, like Email, then press the **Center Button** and tap the "Email" icon to start it up.

Compose a new message and then use the Menu or Gesture Shortcut (Touch + V) to paste the text into an email message.

Deleting a Word at a Time

If you need to quickly erase an entire word, or several words, hold the SHIFT key and press the Backspace Key.

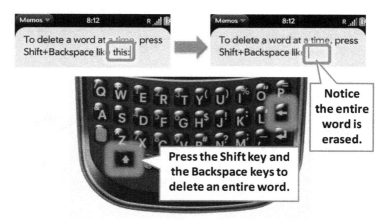

Universal Search

A great thing about the Pre is that if you start typing just about anywhere, (Launcher, Home Screen (with or without Cards showing), Contacts, Web Browser, Contacts, Memos, Tasks and more) a Universal Search window will appear with your search characters. The function of where and what is searched is 'context sensitive.'

Searching Inside Icons

For example, if you are inside Contacts, typing a few letters, SPACE, and a few more letters will search in your Contact List for matching names. In the image we typed "ma" hit SPACE and "t" to show all first names that start with "Ma" and last names that start with "T"

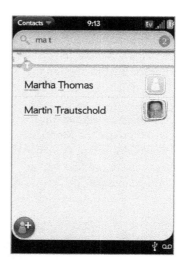

Similarly, typing a few letters in the Phone will also search for matching names. If you type letters in your Memos or Tasks, entries with matching characters (anywhere in the entry) will

appear.
Searching from the Launcher or Card View – Looking for Contacts

Now, if we type the same exact keys ("ma t") starting from our Home Screen or Launcher, we also see matching contact entries.

Simply tap either entry to view their contact information.

Now you can instantly call, email, map their address, add a reminder, or text them, depending on how much information you have stored in their entry.

Searching from the Launcher or Card View – Instant Web Search

The other thing you can do with the Universal Search from the Launcher or Home Screen is perform a web search, Google Maps search, Wikipedia or Twitter search. (More options are likely to be added soon.)

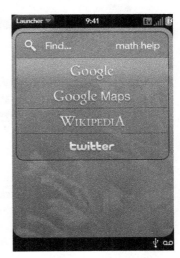

This will save you a lot of time doing web searches.

Let's say we wanted to find "math help" for our child to do their homework.

Then tap "Google" to perform a Google search for "math help."

Almost instantly we have our search results and are able to get our answers. This is a fantastic feature and will save you time.

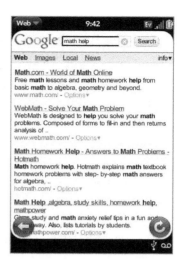

Searching from the Launcher or Card View – Search Google Maps

Let's say you wanted to quickly find local pizza restaurants.

Simply start typing 'pizza' from the Launcher or Home Screen and tap **Google Maps** from the list.

Since your Palm Pre knows your location (from GPS and Location Services), you will instantly see a screen showing you all the local Pizza restaurants.

From this screen you can use the arrows to see the next search results or tap the name of the pizza restaurant to call them or get directions. Learn all about Google Maps in our mapping chapter on page 288.

Chapter 2:
Setup & Synergy

In this chapter we will cover how you get up and running with your Palm Pre. You will learn about your **Palm Profile,** learn the ins and outs of using the new web-sync technology of **Synergy™** and how to transfer your contacts and calendar onto your Pre with the **Data Transfer Assistant**. (Jump to page 57 to learn about Synergy.) Understanding how Synergy works is important to getting the most out of your Pre and understanding what contact and calendaring systems work best with the Pre.

Setting Up Your Pre for the First Time

NOTE: For many people, this first step may have already been performed in the store when the phone was purchased and activated.

Press the "Power" button to turn on the phone, if it is not already on. Slide out the Keyboard and you will begin to see instructions on the screen.

Set the Language

The first thing you need to do is set the "Language" of the device. Just tap the correct language. Your Pre will then check settings and activate itself on the network.

Once activated, you will be prompted to touch the "Next" button, after which you will be taken to a page where you need to read the service agreement and touch "Accept."

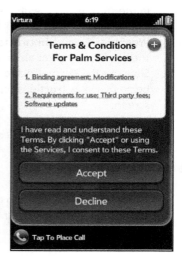

Set up Your "Palm Profile"

The Palm Profile is the required first step to get your phone setup. Every Palm Pre has its own Palm Profile regardless of which service or software is used for email, contacts or calendar. Your Palm Profile will be used to backup, and if necessary later restore, data to your Pre. You can also access your Profile online to erase all data and settings from your Pre in case you lost it or it was stolen. See page 68 to learn how to access your profile from your computer. On page 63, we show you how to get all your important data (contacts, calendars, etc) into your Palm Profile using the Data Transfer Assistant.

Now, you need to set up your Palm Profile – to do this, you must have an active Email account – this will become the "primary" email account associated with the device.

Don't worry, you can set up many more email accounts – we show you how to do this on page 171.

Type in your First and Last Name and then enter a password in the appropriate field. Passwords need to be between 6 and 20 characters. We suggest using a mix of numbers and upper/lowercase letters for greater security.

Next, type in the primary email address for your account. This should be the email address you use most and remember, since you will need to use it to log into your Palm Profile in the future.

Once your profile is created, touch the "Next" button to move to Location Services setup.

Set up Location Services

Location Services uses your GPS location (Global Positioning System satellite fix on your phone's latitude and longitude) to help a particular program find relevant criteria near where you are. For example, if you are in the "Fandango" App looking for a movie, "**Location Services**" will know **where you are** and find theaters nearby.

To enable "**Location Services**," read the agreement and touch "**Agree.**"

Enable "Auto Locate"

You have the option to either enable "**Auto Locate**" which always knows where you are – or tell the Pre to "**Ask Before Locating**" each time an application wants to find information nearby.

NOTE: Using "**Auto Locate**" can put a drain on the battery – we suggest trying the "**Ask Before Locating**" option to preserve Battery Life.

Touch the "Next" button and you will be taken through the Screen Gesture tutorial. If you have not already done so, please check out our Getting Started Guide on page 22 or a full explanation of all the available gestures.

Synergy™ Overview

Why Understand Synergy First?

We describe **Synergy™** before the **Data Transfer Assistant**, because understanding the options provided by Synergy will help you make correct decisions to the questions posed to you in the Data Transfer Assistant. If you want to jump to the Data Transfer Assistant, go to page 63.

Synergy™ is a term Palm has coined to describe the wireless sync capabilities of the new webOS™ software. In a nutshell, Synergy™ means that you can, for the first time on a Smartphone, wirelessly synchronize ("sync"), link and organize all your contact information from different sources (or "services") on the web and keep it in one place – in your "Contacts" and "Calendar" Apps on the Pre.

You will be amazed by how the Pre syncs, automatically links and organizes your contact information from web-based applications (like Google™, facebook™, LinkedIn™). We predict more web-based services such as Yahoo! and others will be added time goes on.

With **Third Party Sync** applications, you can extend the capabilities of Synergy to synchronize your stand alone desktop applications such as MS Outlook™ (not connected to an Enterprise Server), ACT! By Sage, iCal, Entourage, other applications, or even your trusty old Palm Desktop Software.

How Synergy Works

Probably the easiest way to get a feel for "**Synergy™**" is to watch what happens as you enable (log into one and then two or more accounts on your Pre). This will give you a 'real world example' for how everything works together. See page 57 to learn how to login to your web-based accounts.

Login to One Web-Based Account:

After logging into your Google (Gmail) account on your Pre, your Google Contacts and Calendar will flow automatically into the Pre Contacts and Calendar icons.

Login to Another Web-Based Account:

Next, if you log into your facebook™ account, you will see all your Friends appear in your Contact icon, and any facebook calendar events appear on your Pre Calendar. (Usually showing on your Calendar as a different color.)

Login to a Third Web-Based Account:

Maybe you also happen to use LinkedIn or you may use Microsoft Outlook tied to an Exchange™ Email Server, then you will also see all those contacts and calendar also appear on your Pre.

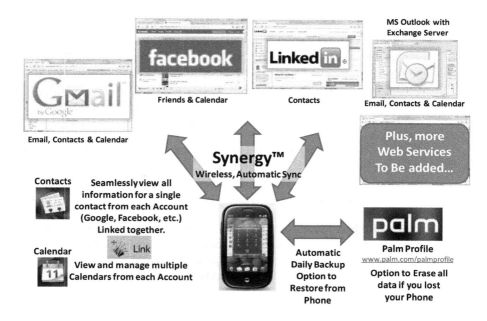

Merged Contact Information – "Linked But Separate"

Let's say you have the same individual in your Google contacts and as a friend in Facebook. You will notice that in your Pre Contacts Icon, you should only see a single contact entry with all the Google Information seamlessly linked together with the Facebook information. If that person has a picture associated with their contact in Google or facebook, the great thing is that you will see their picture right next to their name.

How Contact Linking Works

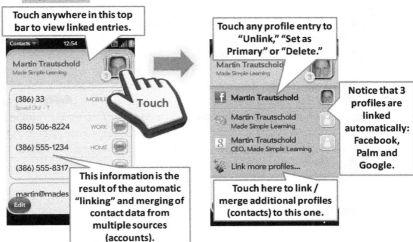

The image above shows that Martin Trautschold happens to have three profiles linked together. (facebook™, Palm Profile and Google™)

NOTE: These should be automatically linked as you setup each account, if they are not linked, then you can manually link them by touching the Top Gray bar and selecting "Link more profiles…"

The nice thing about this linking inside your Palm Contacts icon is that you no longer see duplicates and you get to see all the information merged together in a single set of data for that individual. If you have someone's email address from facebook and their phone number from your Palm Profile, you will see them all together in a single place under the correct contact where you would expect them. Why aren't all Smartphones this smart?

All this works well if you use one or more of these online services, but not everyone is setup this way.

What if I don't use Google, facebook or Outlook connected to Microsoft Exchange today for my contacts and calendar?

You have a few choices:

Option 1: Start using one or more of the online web apps that sync with the Pre (e.g. Google, facebook, LinkedIn)

Google is probably the most complete web-based solution that works seamlessly with the Pre Synergy™ feature today that includes Contacts, Calendar and Email. Facebook is great for contacts, but the built in 'event calendar' is not designed for the individual user. LinkedIn is also great for contacts but currently lacks a calendar.

If you have your information stored in another application, then you will use the Palm Data Transfer assistant (see page 63). The Data Transfer assistant will transfer your data from your existing application into one of the online services (Google, facebook, etc.) or directly into your Palm Profile. From there, Synergy will take over and keep the contacts in sync with the online service.

We recommend using at least one online service that works with Synergy.
Why? The main reason is that you will be able to edit, add and delete contacts and calendars on the online service (e.g. Google).
In other words, if you decide to use only your Palm Profile (and not any online service), you will only be able to see and update your Contacts and Calendar on your Pre.

Third Party Sync Options
If you love your current desktop application and do not want to stop using it, then you have two more options that will allow you to continue to use your computer application and keep it in sync with your Pre. (This assumes there is a Third Party solution that is compatible with your Desktop Computer software)

The two Third Party Sync options take slightly different approaches:
Option 2: Direct Sync Computer to Pre, or
Option 3: Indirect Sync Computer to Google to Pre
Both of these options require that you acquire (some for free / some for purchase) and install Third Party software to perform the synchronization.

We cannot cover these Third Party sync options in detail in this book due to the changing nature of software and space limitations. We recommend contacting the software vendor and Palm Pre forum sites for assistance and user feedback.

Option 2: Direct Sync Computer Application to Pre

You would select this option if you want to continue to use your computer software application, do not want to setup a Google account (nor have your data pass through Google), and have a supported software application.

Direct Sync Computer to Palm Pre
Use Third Party Software to Sync Directly to your Pre

**Standalone
Computer Applications**

**Third Party
Sync Applications**

The Missing Sync for Palm Pre
www.markspace.com

Supported Applications
(See vendor websites for
latest details)

Chapura Echo
for Palm Desktop
www.chapura.com

Mac: Address Book, iCal,
Entourage, MS Outlook

Chapura PocketMirror
for Outlook
www.chapura.com

Windows: Palm Desktop,
MS Outlook

*** FREQUENT UPDATES *** More solutions are added every month, and some of these may no longer be available. It is likely that there are more solutions than listed below. TO locate the most up-to-date list, perform a web search for **"palm pre sync software"**

Current solutions in this category are:
> The Missing Sync for Palm Pre - www.markspace.com
> Chapura Echo for Palm Desktop - www.chapura.com
> Chapura PocketMirror for Outlook - www.chapura.com

Supported computer applications are:
> Mac: Address Book, iCal, Entourage, MS Outlook
> Windows: Palm Desktop, MS Outlook

Option 3: Indirect Sync Computer to Google to Pre
Select this option if you want to continue using your computer software application, are fine with setting up a free Google account and your data passing through Google, and use a supported software application.

Indirect Sync Computer to Google to Palm Pre

Pass-through Sync via Third Party Software and Google/Synergy

Standalone Computer Applications

Gmail™ Account

Third Party Sync Applications

Contacts & Calendar

Selected Applications
(See vendor websites for Latest details)

Google Sync (for iCal, Address Book & Outlook)
http://www.google.com/sync

Synergy™

Wireless, Automatic Sync

<u>Mac:</u> Address Book, iCal, Entourage, MS Outlook, Palm Desktop

CompanionLink for Google (for Outlook, Palm Desktop, ACT! By Sage, Lotus Notes, Novell GroupWise, FrontRange Goldmine)
http://www.companionlink.com/

<u>Windows:</u> ACT! By Sage, IBM Lotus Notes, Novell GroupWise, FrontRange Goldmine, MS Outlook

Sync'Em
(for Outlook, Entourage, Apple Address Book, iCal)
http://www.syncem.com/

Current solutions in this category are:

> Google Sync (for iCal, Address Book & Outlook)
> http://www.google.com/sync
> CompanionLink for Google (for Outlook, Palm Desktop,
> ACT! By Sage, Lotus Notes, Novell GroupWise, FrontRange
> Goldmine)
> http://www.companionlink.com/
> Sync'Em (for Outlook, Entourage, Apple Address Book, iCal)
> http://www.syncem.com/

Supported computer applications are:

> <u>Mac:</u> Address Book, iCal, Entourage, MS Outlook, Palm Desktop
> <u>Windows:</u> ACT! By Sage, IBM Lotus Notes, Novell GroupWise,
> FrontRange Goldmine, MS Outlook

*** FREQUENT UPDATES *** More solutions are added every month, and some of these may no longer be available. It is likely that there are more solutions than listed below. TO locate the most up-to-date list, perform a web search for "**palm pre sync software**"

Data Transfer Assistant

IMPORTANT NOTE: If you already use one of the supported web services such as Google, LinkedIn, facebook or have a Microsoft Exchange-supported Outlook™ for all your contact and calendaring needs, then you can skip the Data Transfer Assistant. You will be doing all your setup using the Palm Pre itself in the Preferences and Accounts section of the Calendar and Contacts icons.

Once your Palm Profile has been created, you will receive an email from Palm with a link to download software that will do an initial "one-time" and "one-way" transfer of information from Microsoft Outlook, Apple iCal or Palm Desktop and move the information into your Pre.

Once the information is moved into your Pre using the Data Transfer Assistant, it will be sent "into the clouds" to your Palm Profile and then stay in sync with changes you make on your Pre.

Without some Third Party software, the data you enter on your Pre will not stay in sync with your desktop application.

NOTE: If you do not use one of the web-based applications (e.g. Google, Facebook, LinkedIn) and want a two-way sync between your Pre and your stand alone computer software, please see page 60.

Check your Email for the "Profile Verification"

Shortly after you create your "**Palm Profile**," your email should arrive with the link to download the required software for your PC or Mac. Open the email from your computer and click the link.

Click the link and then decide which software you need. If you skipped over our section on Synergy™, it would be a good time to check it out starting on page 57. Our Synergy Overview will help you make the decisions below and understand their implications for how you work with your Pre and desktop applications going forward.

If none of the listed options work for you, Palm also provided a link the other "Third Party" options for moving your data (several of which are available in the "App Catalog") on your device. (See page 60 for more on Third Party sync options.)

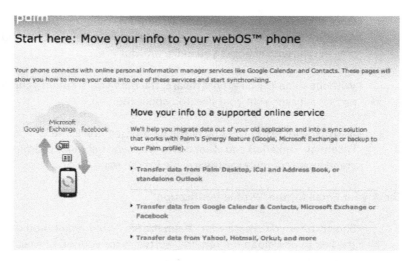

Choose the best software for your needs

Once you have decided on the best option for you (most users will choose either the "Outlook" or "Mac" option), click the highlighted program and then accept all license agreements provided. What this software wants to do is take your data out of your existing (unsupported) desktop application and migrate or copy it to a supported online service (Google, Facebook, etc.).

What if I don't want to stop using my desktop application (Palm Desktop, Outlook, iCal, etc.)?
Don't worry, there are software companies out there that provide applications to allow you to keep using your desktop application and keep it in sync with your phone. See page 60.

> **Move your info to a supported online service**
>
> We'll help you migrate data out of your old application and into a sync solution that works with Palm's Synergy feature (Google, Microsoft Exchange or backup to your Palm profile).
>
> ‣ Transfer data from Palm Desktop, iCal and Address Book, or standalone Outlook
>
> ‣ Transfer data from Google Calendar & Contacts, Microsoft Exchange or Facebook
>
> ‣ Transfer data from Yahoo!, Hotmail, Orkut, and more

Choose a destination for the software – usually called "Data Transfer Assistant."

Start the Data Transfer Assistant

Once you locate the downloaded file, double click on it to start the "**Data Transfer Assistant**"

Follow the on-screen prompts as the "**Data Transfer Assistant**" collects the data from the appropriate source on your computer. When prompted, plug in your Pre™ to the PC or Mac to allow the transfer of data to take place.

Enable "USB Drive" on the Pre™

When you plug in your Pre™ to your computer, you are prompted to choose either "**Media Sync**," "**USB Drive**," or "**Just Charge**." This is the case every time you plug in your Pre™ for purposes of the "**Data Transfer Assistant**," you must choose "**USB Drive**."

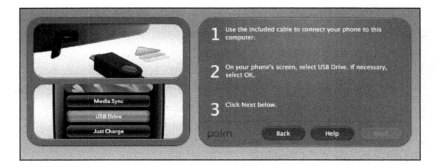

The transfer of your data will then begin. Once the transfer is complete, you will see the final screen of the "**Data Transfer Assistant**" letting you know that your data is now safely on your Pre and part of your "**Palm Profile**."

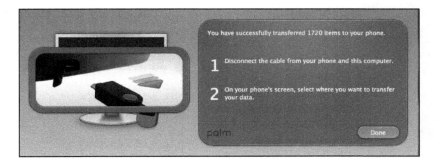

You will then be prompted to disconnect your phone and select where, specifically, you would like your data transferred.

Your choices are your Google or Exchange Account or your Palm Profile.

Transfer to your Google or Exchange Account if:

- You presently use -- or plan to use -- **Google Calendar** and **Google Contacts** to manage your data (see page 70 more information).
- You want to keep your data synchronized between your phone and your desktop application using a Third Party Sync solution. See page 61.
- You are connected to a Microsoft Exchange Server at work – if you are not sure, check with your Technology Support department at your work place. This is primarily for Business or Enterprise users.

Transfer to your Palm Profile if:

- You no longer want to stay in sync between your phone and your desktop application (e.g. Palm Desktop, Outlook standalone, or other software).
- You wish to backup wirelessly with Palm, but don't want all your information sent to the "Google Cloud." (Note: As of publishing time, you could not see, manage or edit your contacts anywhere but on your Pre with this option.)

Once your choice is made, your contacts and information will be transferred to the desired location. Touch the "Transfer Now" button to begin.

How to Log Into Your Palm Profile from Your Computer

NOTE: At publishing time, the only things you could do from the Palm Profile computer web site were: Change your Palm Profile name, email, password, security question and erase your phone. You were not able to browse or see at the stored backup information from your phone (contacts, calendar, etc.) for security purposes.

Go to: www.palm.com/palmprofile from your computer to log in.

At publishing time, clicking this link from your computer got you to a screen that looked like this: (It may look different when you go to it as web sites change frequently.)

Enter the email address and password you used to originally setup your phone.

If you forgot your password, click the "Forgot password?" link under the login box to have your password emailed to you:

Then you must answer the secret question:

If you entered your email address correctly and answered the question correctly, you will then be permitted to reset your password.

After you have successfully logged in, you will see a screen similar to this one:

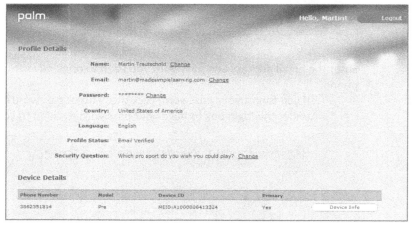

Click on the "**Device Info**" next to your phone shown on the bottom left of the screen above to see this:

If you lost your phone, click the "**I Lost My Phone**" button at the bottom of the web page to erase all the data from your phone -- A great security feature to protect your private information.

A Synergy Sync Example: Google Contacts and Calendar

The great thing about using the Synergy sync to Google for the Palm® Pre™ is that it provides you a full two-way wireless synchronization. What this means is anything you type in on your Google Calendar/Addresses "magically" (wirelessly and automatically) appears on your Pre™ Calendar/Contacts in minutes! (The auto-sync duration was about 15 minutes, but this may change, and you can even 'force a **Sync Now**' to happen in the "Preferences & Accounts" screen on your Pre.) The same thing goes for Contacts or Calendar events you add or change on your Pre™ – they are transmitted wirelessly and automatically to show up on your Google Calendar and Address Book.

NOTE: The only exceptions are those calendar events you have added on your Pre™ prior to enabling the Google Sync inside your "Preferences & Accounts" – those 'old' events don't get synced. Contacts on your Pre™ prior to the Google account activation are synced.

Getting Started with Gmail and Google Calendar on your Computer
First, if you don't already have one, you must sign up for a free Google Mail ("Gmail") account at www.gmail.com.

Then, follow the help and instructions on Google to start adding address book entries and creating calendar events on Gmail and Google Calendar on your computer.

Looking at the Results of a Successful Synergy Sync (Calendar & Contacts)

Google Calendar on the Computer:

Pre™ Calendar:

Notice the calendar events from Google Calendar are now on your Pre™. Anything you add or change on your Pre or Google calendar will be shared both ways going forward. Automatically! The same goes for Google Contacts and Contacts on your Pre.

Google Contacts on your Computer:

Pre™ Contacts:

Chapter 3:
Media Transfer

The Pre was originally designed by Palm to work effortlessly with iTunes when Media Sync mode is enabled. In the ensuing months, Apple and discontinued the sync and Palm has restored it. Because we don't know where this will end up, we are giving you other options for syncing media in this chapter.

If Apple has not disabled the iTunes connection, your Pre looks like another iPod to the iTunes software. (See page 83.)

You can also manually transfer media to your Pre using it as a "Mass Storage Device" via "USB Drive" Mode (see page 79.)

What if I already use an iPod?

You may have a few of these questions:

Can I put all my purchased music on my Palm Pre?   That depends. Any music that is does not have DRM (Digital Rights Management) embedded within can be played on your Pre. Songs purchased before early 2009 on from iTunes and other stores are likely to be DRM protected.

Why is my music being 'skipped' over on the Pre? Why won't it play? If music is protected with DRM, it will appear to transfer and be listed on your Pre in your music library. However, when you go to listen to any DRM song on your Pre, nothing will happen – the Pre will pause for a second and then skip over it to the next song.

Can I keep using my iPod? Yes! You can definitely keep listening to all your music on both your iPod and your new Palm Pre.

Software Alternatives to iTunes for Media Sync (Music, Videos, Pictures)

Since the Pre was designed to sync with iTunes, if that sync is working, you should use it. However, there are many alternatives to iTunes which are quite good and even look, feel and work like iTunes. Some of the popular software alternatives are:

> **doubleTwist™** - www.doubletwist.com – Founded in Oslo, Norway, now headquartered in San Francisco and backed by venture capitalists. With this software, you can sync your Playlists and media, however at publishing time, it did not allow you to edit or create new Playlists. **Price: Free.**
> We cover the basics of using doubleTwist™ in this book.

> **Song Bird™** - www.getsongbird.com - Powered by Mozilla – the developers of the popular Firefox web browser. **Price: Free.**

> **Media Monkey™** - www.mediamonkey.com – Created by Ventis Media – a popular tool for downloading, managing and syncing media. **Price: Free** or $19.95 for the Gold Edition.

*** MORE SOLUTIONS *** - Do a web search for "media sync software palm pre" to find all the latest additions to this category. Also check out the Palm Pre or webOS™ blogs online to learn about user feedback and options.

doubleTwist™ - A Great way to Media Sync to your Pre

> This is one of several software alternatives (see page 74 for more options) to iTunes that work well to sync music, pictures and videos to your Palm Pre. doubleTwist™ it works for many other smartphones and devices in addition to the Pre: BlackBerry, Sony PSP, Google G1, Android phones, Windows Mobile, LG Viewty, iPhone, iPod, many digital cameras, flash memory video recorders, and more.

> Based on their web site, doubleTwist™ is founded on the philosophy of: "A unifying media platform that connects consumers with all their media and all their devices, regardless of whether they are online or offline."

Essentially, doubleTwist will import all your iTunes information – including playlists – and then allow you to drag and drop them right onto your Pre.

doubleTwist also helps you share large media files like videos and high-resolution photos with friends and family. Send baby pictures to Grandma or lots of pictures you've taken on your Pre to your friends.

Download and Install DoubleTwist

The first step to get your media into your Pre using DoubleTwist is to download the application. From your computer, visit: http://www.doubletwist.com/dt/Home/Index.dt and DoubleTwist will be able to tell which version of the software is right for your computer.

There are Mac™ and Windows™ versions!

Download the install file and follow the directions for setup.

For a Mac, just drag the doubleTwist icon to your applications folder.

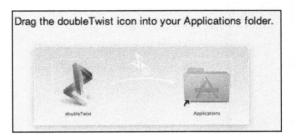

For a Windows PC, "run" the setup program as prompted:

Unless you have one already, you will be prompted to create a doubleTwist account. Type your user name, email and password for a one-time setup of your account.

Does doubleTwist cost anything?

No. At publishing time there were no charges associated with doubleTwist.

A confirmation email will be sent letting you know that your account is now active.

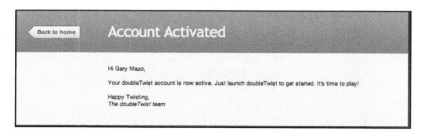

Double click the doubleTwist icon on your desktop to start the program.

Click the "Music" tab under your "Library" and doubleTwist will import your iTunes library and playlists.

You will notice that the doubleTwist screen looks quite familiar if you have been an iTunes™ user. This should help you navigate and use the program if you are already familiar with iTunes.

How to setup an "Automatic Sync" with doubleTwist

Like iTunes, you can setup an "Automatic Sync" or leave it as a "Manual Sync." Below are the steps for the "Auto Sync," if you want to manually sync your playlists or drag and drop music, go to page 79.

Plug your Palm Pre into your computer, and your Pre will show up as a "Device" in the sidebar of the program under the "LIBRARY" tab.

You can select either "USB Drive" or "Media Sync" modes on your Pre.

The first time you plug your Pre in, you will see check boxes asking if you want to sync Pictures, Music, or Videos. You can check one, two or all three.

Note: In order to see these tabbed views, you have to click on the "Palm Pre" under "DEVICES" in the left column as shown.

Once you check a box, then you are given a link to select which folders or playlists to sync. You may also click the tabs at the top to get to the same area to select folders or playlists.

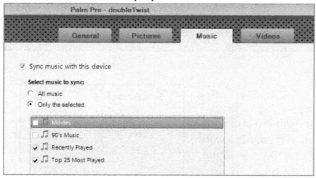

Select "All music" or "Only the selected" for each of the tabs.

When you are done with all your selections, can click the "Sync" button in the lower left corner.

How to Manually Manage Media with doubleTwist

If you choose to manually manage your media (pictures, songs and videos) with doubleTwist, you can simply drag and drop playlists, videos, pictures or entire folders onto your Pre. We have some good tips and tricks on selecting multiple items in a list or individual items not in a list so you can more easily drag and drop – see page 93.

Troubleshooting tips for using doubleTwist:

iTunes is popping up
If you have iTunes installed on your computer, it may pop-up and try to sync with your Pre in "Media Sync" mode. If this happens, close iTunes and return to doubleTwist.

Select "USB Drive"
The other option which may avoid having iTunes pop-up when you connect your Pre is to select "USB Drive" instead of "Media Sync" mode.

Note: If you want doubleTwist to automatically sync your media, go to page 77.

Locate your iTunes playlists in the top window and just grab a playlist and drag it onto your Pre in the left column.

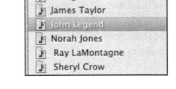

If you need to check on your space for media files, just click on your "Palm Pre" under devices, then click the "General" tab a the top of the screen to see the capacity of your Pre.

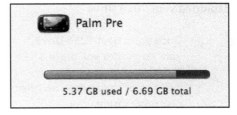

USB Transfer Mode for Media

iTunes or other Third Party software can be great options for Media transfer, but there may be times when you want a different way to get your Media on the Pre (especially if iTunes support gets discontinued.)

Fortunately, your Pre comes with USB transfer mode built in.

Starting the "USB Drive" Mode

Plug your Pre into your computer as you did using the USB cable – see page 73.

When the option screen shows you your three options; "Media Sync, "USB Drive" or "Just Charge" choose the "**USB Drive**" option.

USB Warning – No Phone calls or Text Messages

You may receive a warning message when you first choose "**USB Drive**" – alerting you to the fact that you cannot use your phone or receive calls or messages while connected in this mode.

Just choose "OK" and continue.

Exploring your "USB Drive"

Once you select "USB Drive," your computer will place a "USB" icon on your Mac desktop or show up as another disk drive inside your Windows™ Explorer.

Double click the icon or disk drive and you will see the file structure of the Pre.

Add a "Music" folder

To help keep your Music organized on your Pre, we suggest that you add a new folder in the window and call it "Music." On a Windows machine, just right click and choose "New Folder" and on a Mac, go up to the "file" Menu in "Finder" and select "New Folder." Name the folder "Music."

untitled folder

Rename to....

Music

Double click the folder (it should be empty) and minimize it – you will need it later.

Transferring your Music or Videos

Navigate to the folder where you store music on your computer. In this example, we are on a Mac (but Windows works in a similar way).

Inside the "Music" folder we see an iTunes folder and once we double-click that, we see the iTunes Music folder.

iTunes Music

Copy and Paste Media

Find the "Folder" containing the song or music you are seeking. Most MP3 media programs store your music in folders, often with separate files for the Album Art. (Picture of the cover of the Album/CD).

In this example, we want to copy the full album of Bruce Springsteen entitled "Working on a Dream." We first find the "Bruce Springsteen" folder and look through all the albums and their folders.

There is one folder entitled "Working on a Dream" and it contains the full album with all the album art. We highlight the folder and either "right click" or go up to the "Edit" menu and select "Copy."

Now, we go back to that minimized window of the new "Music" folder on the Pre itself. We either "right click" or go to the "edit" menu and select "Paste" to copy this album on to the Pre.

The contents of the folder including all songs and album art will now be transferred to the Pre.

Finding the Album on the Pre

Start the Music Icon on the Pre and select "Albums."

Using the keyboard, start typing the name of the album – in this case – "working" is enough to find the album we want: "Working on a Dream."

The album should appear. Touch the icon of the album and you should see all the songs from that album with the "Album Art" intact.

NOTE: You can use this "**USB Drive**" technique to transfer all the music you would like – providing you don't exceed the available memory on the Pre. You can also make a folder just like you did on page 80 called "**Videos**" and copy and paste video files on your Pre.

Using iTunes to Sync Media to your Pre

If you have iTunes Installed Already, Check Your Current Version

If you have already installed iTunes, you should check which version you currently have. The easiest was to do that is start up your iTunes program, go to "Help" (on your PC) or iTunes (farthest menu to the left on the Mac) and then to "About iTunes." You will see right here that the version number of your particular version is shown. If you don't have version 9.0 or higher – it is time to upgrade.

NOTE: As we mentioned, Apple and Palm have been doing a little "Cat and Mouse" game with iTunes support. It is possible that iTunes may not work with the Pre forever – which is why we also cover Third Party Sync applications (page 74) and USB transfer mode (see page 79.) Probably the best way to find what is working is to either do a web search for "palm pre sync software" or check one of the Palm Pre blog sites such as www.precentral.net.

NOTE: With iTunes, you can synchronize music, videos, TV shows, podcasts, and pictures, but you cannot sync iTunes contacts, calendar events, or games.

Download iTunes from the Apple Web site

If you decide you need to download and install the latest version of iTunes, go to www.itunes.com/download. This link works equally well for both PC and Mac users and download and install the latest version of the software.

Running iTunes the First Time - the "Setup Assistant"

If you are just running iTunes for the first time on your computer, you will be asked a few questions by the "**iTunes Setup Assistant**" to help iTunes work better for you.

WARNING: Choosing "Yes" will cause videos, music and other media in separate directories to be moved out of these directories into the iTunes directory causing other programs that access this media to no longer function correctly!

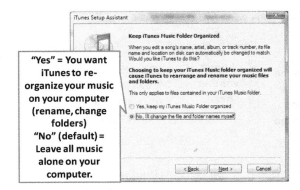

"Yes" = You want iTunes to re-organize your music on your computer (rename, change folders)
"No" (default) = Leave all music alone on your computer.

iTunes Basics - Playing Songs, Videos and More

If you are new to iTunes, there are a few basic pointers on how to get around.

Playing a Song or Video: Just double-click on it to start playing it.

Controlling the Song or Video: Use the Rewind, Pause, Fast-Forward Buttons and Volume Slider in the upper left corner to control the playback.

Moving to a different part of the Song or Video: Click on the diamond in slider bar under the song name in the top of the window and drag it left or right as desired.

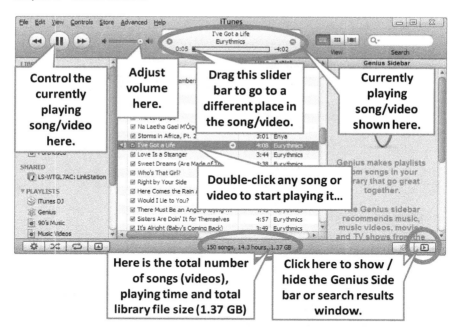

Control the currently playing song/video here.

Adjust volume here.

Drag this slider bar to go to a different place in the song/video.

Currently playing song/video shown here.

Double-click any song or video to start playing it...

Here is the total number of songs (videos), playing time and total library file size (1.37 GB)

Click here to show / hide the Genius Side bar or search results window.

iTunes Basics - Creating a New Playlist

You may be used to listening to all the music on a particular Album, but you will soon find the benefits of creating your own custom Playlists. These are lists of particular songs that you group together.

Playlists could be any grouping you like for example:

- Workout Music
- Favorite U2 Songs
- Traveling Music

To create a new playlist, you can press "**Ctrl + N**", select "**New Playlist**" from the "**File**" menu, or simply click the **New Playlist button** in the lower left corner of iTunes, as shown. Then type the name

Click here to create a new Playlist...

Then type your Playlist name here.

of your playlist.

Now, you need to find music to add to your new Playlist. To select from your entire library, click "Music" under the Library tab.

To select songs from a Playlist already created, click on that playlist.

Adding Individual Songs:

Click on any individual song to select it, then keep holding down the mouse key while you drag it over to your new Playlist. To put it into the playlist, "drop it," by letting go of the mouse key when the song name you are dragging is on the Playlist name.

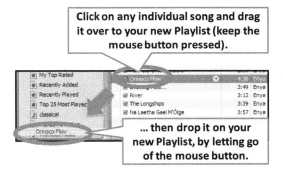

Adding Multiple Songs/Videos:

1. To add selected songs that are not all listed together, press and hold the CTRL key (Windows) or COMMAND key (Mac), then click on

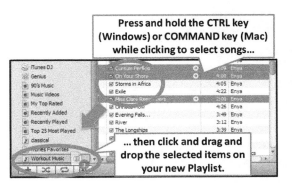

individual songs/videos. Once you are done selecting songs/videos, then release the CONTROL/COMMAND key.

2. After all the songs/videos are selected (highlighted), click on one of the selected songs and drag and drop the entire selected group onto your Playlist.

Adding a List of Songs/Videos:

1. To add a list of songs/videos that are all together in a continuous list, press and hold the SHIFT key. Then while pressing the SHIFT key, click on the top item in the list, then click on the bottom item. All items will be selected.

Press and hold the SHIFT key and click on the top item...

...while holding SHIFT, click on the bottom item to select the entire list.

After the list is selected, let go of SHIFT key then click to drag and drop the list on to your Playlist.

2. After all the songs/videos are selected (highlighted), click on one of the selected songs and drag and drop the entire selected group onto your Playlist.

Connecting Your Palm Pre to iTunes the First Time

Once you have iTunes set up and running on your computer and your Playlists organized, you are ready to connect your Palm Pre for the first time.

Plug in the USB connection cable that was supplied with your Palm Pre to a USB port on your computer.

Choose "**Media Sync**" from the choices given to you.

iTunes should start automatically when you select "Media Sync." If it does not start automatically, double-click it on your computer to start it.

Can I sync using Bluetooth instead of the USB cable?

No. At the time of publishing, Bluetooth transfer speeds were too slow to allow syncing of your media to your Palm Pre, so Bluetooth connection for iTunes Sync is not allowed.

Windows will install the necessary drivers and then iTunes will launch the new Palm Pre setup screen.

iTunes sees your Palm® Pre™ as an iPod® – so, don't panic when it says "Set up your iPod." You should see the name "Palm Pre" in the name box.

Give your Palm Pre a name. Each time you plug in your Palm Pre – to this or any other computer – your Palm Pre will show the name you choose here.

Name: Palm Pre

We will name this one simply **"Palm Pre."**

You will also see two boxes available to check – one is to automatically sync songs to your Palm Pre, the other is to automatically sync photos. If you want all of your music that is in your iTunes library on your new Palm Pre – then go ahead and check that box. *WARNING: Your Palm Pre does not have as much memory as your computer, so be careful selecting "automatically sync" when you have 1,000's of songs in your computer iTunes library.*

☐ Automatically sync songs to my iPod
iTunes can automatically sync your iPod to mirror its music library and playlists each time you connect it to this Mac.

☐ Automatically add photos to this iPod
iTunes will first sync all of your music to your iPod and then use the remaining space for photos. If all of your photos will not fit, they will be copied in the order specified in the Photos pane of iPod preferences.

If you like to manage your music on your own or your Palm Pre cannot hold your entire music library from iTunes, then don't check this "Automatically Sync Songs" box.

Follow the same rule of thumb with your pictures: if you want all your pictures on your Palm Pre or all pictures from a particular folder, then go ahead and check this box – otherwise, leave it blank and you can manually add pictures later on.

Once you confirm your choices, you will be taken to the main screen that you will see every time you connect your Palm Pre to iTunes.

Create an iTunes Account or Sign In (Required to Buy Anything)

If you have music CDs that you want to load onto your Palm Pre using iTunes, then check out our section for loading CDs on page 92. If you want to buy songs, videos and more, you will need to purchase them from the iTunes store.

In order to Sign In or create a new iTunes account, you will need to click the "Sign In" button in the upper right corner as shown below.

If you do not yet have an iTunes account, then click the "Create New Account" button and follow the instructions to create your new account. If you already have an account, then entering your Apple ID or AOL screen name and password, then click the "**Sign In**" button.

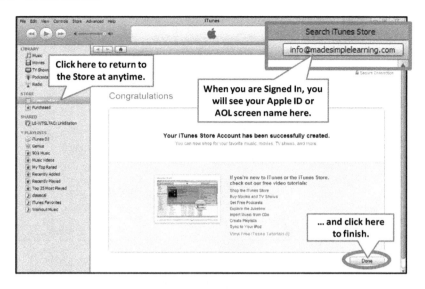

Loading My Music CDs into iTunes so I can put them on my Palm Pre

If you have Music CDs that you want to load up onto your Palm Pre, you will need to first load them into iTunes, then use the methods we describe in this book to move them to your Palm Pre. (See page 96 for "Auto Sync" or page 93 for the "Drag and Drop" method.)

First, start up iTunes. Then, insert the CD into your computer's CD drive. You may see a pop-up inside iTunes that asks if you would like to import the CD as shown.

Click "Yes" to import the CD.

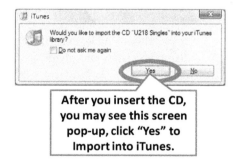

After you insert the CD, you may see this screen pop-up, click "Yes" to Import into iTunes.

If you did not receive this pop-up window, then you can manually start the CD import into iTunes by clicking the Import CD button in the lower right corner. You will also notice that the CD has appeared under the "DEVICES" list in the left column.

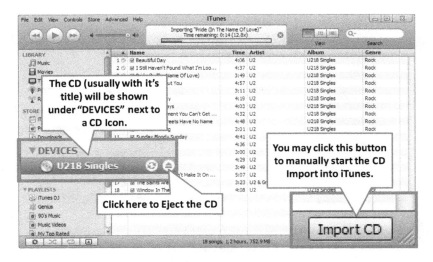

Now you have successfully imported the CD into your Music Library in iTunes, you will need to add these items to a Playlist that is setup to sync to your Palm Pre (see page 96), or you can manually "Drag and Drop" some or all of these songs to your Palm Pre (see page 93).

Manually Putting Music and Playlists in iTunes ("Drag & Drop" Method)

If you chose to "manually" sync your music (by leaving the "Automatically Sync" checkbox unchecked) -- you will then have to drag and drop songs, videos or Playlists onto your Palm Pre to get music or videos onto the Palm Pre.

When your Palm Pre is connected, you will see it listed in the left hand column under "Devices."

Use the same techniques as we showed above when you added songs to a new Playlist to add songs to your Palm Pre.

SELECTING AND MOVING SONGS (NOT IN A LIST):

Once you have found music that you want to put onto your Palm Pre. Select the songs (or albums) by holding down the "Ctrl" button

(Windows) or "Command" button (Mac) while using your mouse and left-click (Single click for Mac) on each song. The highlighted songs will turn blue.

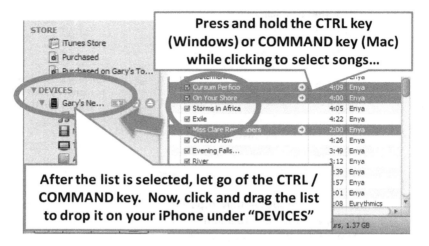

Press and hold the CTRL key (Windows) or COMMAND key (Mac) while clicking to select songs...

After the list is selected, let go of the CTRL / COMMAND key. Now, click and drag the list to drop it on your iPhone under "DEVICES"

SELECTING AND MOVING SONGS/VIDEOS IN A LIST:
To highlight an entire album or many songs listed in a row – for example all songs by a particular artist – hold down the "Shift" key (Windows and Mac)   and click (left-click in Windows) the top of the list – then go all the way to the bottom of the list you want to copy – go to the last song (keeping the shift key held down) and left click again. All the songs between those two points will turn blue.

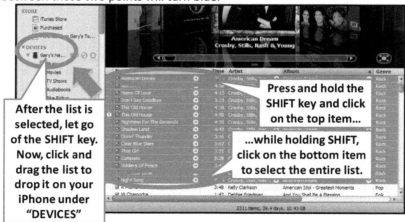

After the list is selected, let go of the SHIFT key. Now, click and drag the list to drop it on your iPhone under "DEVICES"

Press and hold the SHIFT key and click on the top item...

...while holding SHIFT, click on the bottom item to select the entire list.

Now, click and hold down the Mouse button (left button for Windows) and "Drag" all the highlighted songs to your Palm Pre, listed under "Devices." You will see the information window detail the transfer from iTunes to your Palm Pre.

Manually Transferring Videos within iTunes

The process to manually add or remove Movies, TV Shows, Podcasts is the same as we show on page 93 to manually transfer songs to your Palm Pre.

Example:
To transfer a specific movie you would:

1. Click on the "Movies" tab in the left column under "LIBRARY" to see your movies.

2. Click and drag a single movie or several selected movies (learn how to select multiple movies in a row or separately on page 93) and drop it on your Palm Pre under DEVICES.

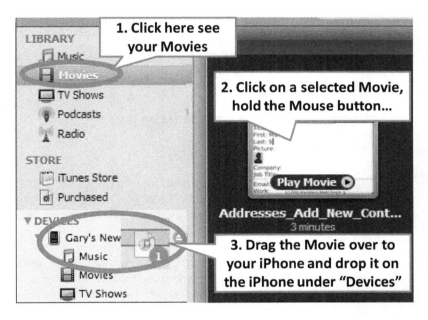

3. Once the movie (or movies) have been 'dropped' on your Palm Pre then just press the "Sync" button at the bottom right and the selected media will be synced right to my Palm Pre.

Why might I not want to use iTunes "Automatic Sync"?

There could be a few reasons to manually sync, but the primary one is this: If you put all your Music, Videos, etc. onto your Palm Pre you will run out of room for important stuff like: your email and all those fun Apps from the App catalog!

Automatically Synchronizing your iTunes Music and Videos to your Palm Pre

If you selected the "Automatically Synchronize" as shown on page 90, you will see a "Updating files on Palm Pre" message window at the top if iTunes showing you the status of the sync process.

Updating Files on "Palm Pre"
Copying 13 of 40: Running On Empty

Click here
to stop
and cancel
the sync.

How can I stop the iTunes Sync process to my Palm Pre?

Sometimes you might want to cancel the sync process to your Palm Pre. To cancel the sync click the small "x" in the upper right hand corner of the Synchronize window.

Can I play my iTunes Purchased media on my Pre?

The short answer is **"Maybe."**

The answer is **"NO"** for all songs purchased on iTunes earlier than January 2009 and all songs purchased with "DRM" (Digital Rights Management) protection. These songs are tied specifically to one person's iPod/Palm Pre.

The answer is **"YES"** for all songs purchased without DRM Protection enabled. Early in 2009, iTunes announced that it would start selling some songs and videos without DRM Protection, which means they could be played on multiple iPods and Palm Pres.

As we, Made Simple Learning, are creators of intellectual property - books and videos, we don't advocate sharing purchased music, please pay the artist, author or video producer what they deserve - so they can keep making great songs, books and videos!

How do I "Get Album Artwork" in iTunes?

iTunes may automatically get the Album Art for most songs and videos, however, if you need to manually retrieve this Artwork, then follow these steps. *NOTE: You will need to already have an iTunes account and login for this to work correctly.*

Start up iTunes and go to the "**Advanced**" menu and select "**Get Album Artwork**"

TIP: Go into the "Advanced" menu in iTunes to "Get Album Artwork"

How to Turn Off or Disable the iTunes "Automatic Sync"

If you had selected "Automatically Synchronize" media and want to turn this feature off, you need to go into iTunes see page 96.

Finding Songs and Videos Using the Search Box in iTunes

If your library is not already hundreds or thousands of songs and other media, it will be soon! How do you quickly find that special song you are in the mood for right now? The quickest way to locate an individual song or video is to use the "Search" bar in the upper right corner of iTunes.

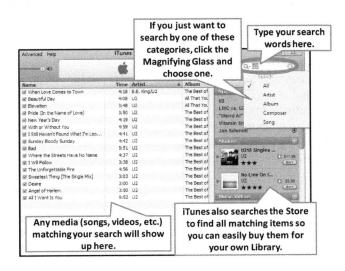

If you just want to search by one of these categories, click the Magnifying Glass and choose one.

Type your search words here.

Any media (songs, videos, etc.) matching your search will show up here.

iTunes also searches the Store to find all matching items so you can easily buy them for your own Library.

In the Search window Just start typing any part of the following categories to find the item:

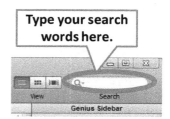

Type your search words here.

- Artist Name
- Album Name
- Composer
- Song/Video Name

You will notice that as soon as you type the first letter, iTunes will narrow your search results (shown in the main window) by that letter.

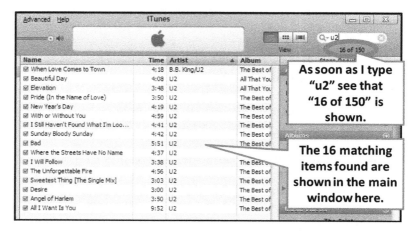

As soon as I type "u2" see that "16 of 150" is shown.

The 16 matching items found are shown in the main window here.

What it is doing is finding all matching songs/videos that have the letter (or series of letters) matching any part of the Artist, Album, Composer or Song/Video name.

SEARCH TIP

You can type any combination of words to match the item you are trying to find. For example, if you know that the song has the word "Love" in the title and the song is by the Artist "U2" - you would just type in the two words separated by a SPACE: "Love U2" and immediately be shown all matching items. In this case, only 2 songs matched, so I can quickly double click on the song I wanted to listen to.

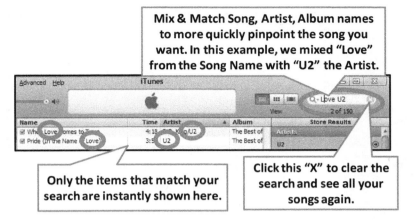

Mix & Match Song, Artist, Album names to more quickly pinpoint the song you want. In this example, we mixed "Love" from the Song Name with "U2" the Artist.

Only the items that match your search are instantly shown here.

Click this "X" to clear the search and see all your songs again.

When you are done searching, just hit the little "X" in the circle next to the search words to clear out the search and see all your songs and videos again.

Transferring Photos with iTunes

If I click on the "Photos" tab, I will see a radio box I can check to sync my photos from a particular folder. In Windows, the default is usually "My Pictures" but I can use the drop down menu to select the correct program in which to find my photo library.

I can then choose to sync all my photos (which would be way too many for my Palm Pre) or just selected folders. Each folder and the number of pictures inside are listed for me to check.

Once I select the photos I wish to Sync, I can just press the "Sync" button and they will be transferred to my Palm Pre.

Chapter 4:
Phone Basics

The Palm Pre is capable of so many things that it is often easy to forget the fact that it is also a phone. The Palm Pre is packed with features you would expect from a high-end Smartphone.

Getting Started with Phone Features

The Palm Pre initially places the Phone icon at the furthest left point of the Quick Launch Bar. You can move this icon somewhere else, just look at "Moving Icons" on page 242.

Tap the "Phone" icon and you will be taken into your Phone App.

The dial pad is front and center. At the top is the Address book icon for making a call from contacts.

At the bottom of the screen are the

"Voicemail"

and

"Call Log" icons.

Finding Your Pre's Phone Number

If you have just received the Palm Pre and it has a new phone number, you will want to know how to find its phone number.

To do this, touch the Phone Icon to start it.

Touch the menu in the upper left corner.

Select **"Preferences"**

Your Pre's phone number is on the top of Preferences screen.

Dialing Using the Keypad

Dial the phone as you would normally. After you start dialing, the "Call Button" is the green phone icon right below the dial pad.

When you are done dialing, tap the Call button at the bottom of the keypad to start the call.

TIP: There is a "Backspace" button in the top right hand corner. If you make a mistake, touch this button to erase the last digit dialed.

TIP: You can also use the number keys from your physical keyboard instead of the on-screen keypad.

Placing Calls from Contacts

One of the great things about having all your contact information in your phone is that it is very easy to place calls from your "Contacts" on the Palm Pre.

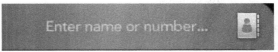

The easiest way to do this is to start the "**Phone**" App and then touch the "Contacts" icon in the top right hand corner.

Either begin to type a name on the keyboard, or just scroll through your contacts to find the right number.

Just touch the number you wish to dial – if a contact has several numbers, just touch the one you want to call. As soon as you touch the number, the phone call will be initiated.

Setting "Speed Dial" on your Palm Pre

It is much easier to save frequently called numbers to "Speed Dial" than have to search through your contacts each time you want to call the frequently called contact.

Adding Your "Speed Dial Numbers"

Speed dialing on the Pre™ is set up in the "Contact" information –not from the Phone application itself.

Touch the "Contacts" icon and either type a few letters of their last and first name to "FIND" the contact or scroll to the appropriate contact.

TIP: if you make a mistake typing the contact name, press the "backspace" key on the keyboard and correct your mistake.

If the contact has more than one number associated with it, they will all be displayed in the contact view.

Tap the top left corner or swipe down in the same place to see the "Contacts Menu."

Tap the "**Set Speed Dial**" menu item.

If the contact has more than one phone number, the next screen will ask you which number – mobile, work or home you wish to set as the "Speed Dial."

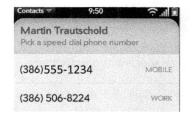

The next screen shows you the available options for "Speed Dial" numbers. NOTE: the number "1" is reserved for your voicemail. Just touch the number slot for this particular contact. In this example, I touched the "T" (3/T) button for Martin Trautschold's "Work" number. Now you can see that reflected in his contact information.

TIP: You have up to 25 letters to assign as Speed Dials!

Calling Your "Speed Dial" Numbers

You can access Speed Dial letters from your Home Screen, Launcher or the Phone App, but you cannot Speed Dial from inside other application icons. In any of these places, simply press and hold the "Speed Dial" Key on the keyboard for the contact you wish to call.

NOTE: While it is tempting to use the on-screen keypad inside the Phone App to speed dial, this will not work correctly. You must use the letters and numbers on **Pre's physical keyboard** – not the Phone on-screen keypad.

To Edit or Reassign a "Speed Dial"

Follow the steps above for setting a speed dial. If you choose a slot already assigned to a speed dial, you will see a message at the bottom saying "Reassign to…." Just touch the "reassign" button and the speed dial will now be set to the new number.

To "Cancel" a "Speed Dial" selection

Start the **Contacts Icon** and touch the "MENU" in the left hand corner.

Choose "Set Speed Dial" as you did above.

Next, touch the number that is already set to a "Speed Dial."

Confirm that you wish to "Remove" the Speed Dial number and it will be removed. You will now notice in the Contact information that the "Speed Dial" indicator is no longer present.

Free Tips and Video Tutorials at www.MadeSimpleLearning.com

Using "Call History"

Using "Call History" is like looking at
your "Call Log" on other smartphones.

When you touch the "Call History" icon,
a list of all your recent calls will be
listed. You can touch the "**All Calls**" or
"**Missed Calls**" button at the top to
narrow down the list.

To Place a Call from "Call History"

Simply touch the name and the Palm Pre
will immediately begin to initiate a phone
call to the individual.

To See Contact Info from "Call History"

In addition to "Calling Back" a number or
contact from your "Call History," you can
also look at the contact information for
that particular contact. To do this, touch
the picture or place holder for the picture
on the right side of each entry.

You will see a new "Card" open up with
the Contact Information from that caller.

What if I Cannot See My Call History or Voicemail Buttons?

As soon as you dial a single digit on the keypad, you will notice that the Call History and Voicemail Buttons are replaced by the "Add to Contacts" button. To get the Call History and Voicemail buttons back, you need to erase all digits dialed with either the on-screen backspace key (upper right corner) or the keyboard backspace key.

Clear Out all or individual "Call History" Items

To clear or erase all your recent call history entries, from the "Call History" screen, touch the MENU in the upper left hand corner and then touch "**Clear Call History.**"

You can also erase individual entries by "Sliding" them to the side and then touching the red "**Delete**" button.

Adding Phone Numbers to Your Contacts from the Phone

There are a couple of ways to add phone numbers to your Contact list in the Pre. You can add a number as you are dialing it, or add any entry from your Call History.

Add from Keypad (Dialed Number)

To add a phone number you have dialed, tap the "**Add to Contacts**" button at the bottom of the keypad as shown.

Then follow the steps shown below in the "Add from Call History" section to either add this as a new contact entry or add this phone number as a new number for an existing contact.

Add from Call History (Call received, placed or missed)

If you have an entry in your Call History that you want to add as a contact

in on your Pre, simply press the "+" in the box  next to the call log
entry.

You are then taken to a screen
where you see the phone number.
Tap the "Add to Contacts" button at
the bottom of the screen.

Now you are given a choice as to
how to add this phone number.
Choose "Save as New" if this person
is not already in your Contact list or
select "Add to Existing" if this is a
new phone number for an existing
contact. Then you will be shown
the Contact list to find the existing
contact.

***I have multiple accounts (Profiles) linked to my Pre, to which profile is
this new contact added?***

Any new contacts are added to
your **Default Account**.

You can view this and change
the Default Account if you bring
up the Menu in Contacts and
select "Preferences & Accounts"

Look at the bottom of the screen
for the "**Default Account**" – in
this case the default account
happens to be Google. TIP: To
change this, tap it and select
another account.

Answering a Call

If the phone is **"open,"** you will see a picture of your caller (if you have a "Caller ID" picture in their Contact entry,) and a **Green phone button** to "Answer" the call below the picture on the left and a **Red "Ignore the call" button** to the right of that.

TIP: The Red button will send the caller immediately to Voicemail.

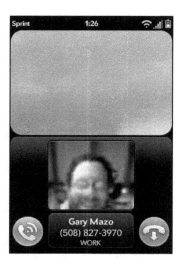

If the phone is **"Closed"** and asleep, you will see the time at the top of the screen, a picture of the caller below that and only a "Green" phone button.
Either drag the "Green" phone button up or just slide open the phone to answer.

Ignoring a Call

Sometimes, you just can't take the call that comes in on the phone. If you are working on your phone and it is "Open," just touch the "Red" ignore button and the call will go to voicemail.

NOTE: If the phone is "Closed" and asleep, you may need to press the "Power" button at the top right of the phone twice to ignore the call.

Silencing the Ringer on a Call

If a call comes in and you have to silence the ringer, you have three options:
- Press either "Volume" button

- Press the "Power" button once (remember, pressing it twice will ignore the call)
- Slide the "Ringer" switch on the top of the phone to the "Off" position

Options While on a Call

All the phone options available to you are clearly indicated in the "Options" screen once a call is initiated.

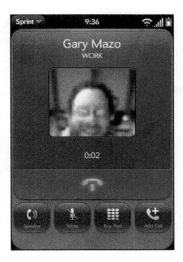

Why does the screen go blank when I hold the phone to my ear?
When you are talking into the Palm Pre holding the phone next to your face, the screen senses this and goes blank so you can't accidentally press a button with your face. The fancy name for this is a "proximity sensor." As soon as you move the Palm Pre away from your face, you will see the options.

Muting the Call

As the number is dialing, you will see the option in the bottom row. To "Mute" the call. Tap the **"Mute"** button to mute yourself.   Press again to un-mute.

Using the Keypad

Perhaps the number you call requires you to then input an extension. Or, perhaps you are calling an automated answering service that requires you to input numbers for choices.

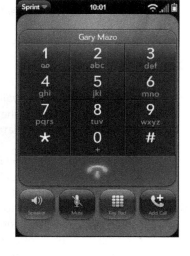

In these situations, touch the "**Keypad**" icon and the keypad will be displayed. Type any digits.

Then press the "**Keypad**" button once again when you are done.

Using the Speaker Phone

If you would prefer to use the built in Speaker Phone on the Palm Pre, just touch the "**Speaker**" icon.

Tap that same icon again to turn off the Speakerphone.

Setting up and Using Voicemail

Your Voicemail icon is always at the bottom left of the screen when in the "Phone" app. Touch the icon for the first time, and you will be prompted to record your voicemail greeting.

Setting up "Standard" voicemail

When you touch your "**Voicemail**" icon for the first time, you will be asked to call your voice mailbox and choose a password and record a greeting. Just follow the voice prompts.

Once your Voicemail is set up, just touch the Voicemail icon to call and retrieve Voicemail in the future.

Playing your Voicemail

Press the "**Voicemail**" icon and the Pre™ will connect to your voicemail – follow the prompts to listen to your messages.

To Hear Message through the Speaker

If you would like to hear your voicemail through the Palm Pre's speaker (as opposed to listening through the handset) just touch the "**Speaker**" button on the bottom row.

Redialing the Last Number Called

Start you "Phone" App as usual by touching the Phone icon in the "Quick Launch Bar." Touch the "**Green Phone**" button and the name of the last person dialed will appear on the top line.

Touch the Green phone button a second time, and the call to the previous caller will be re-dialed.

Chapter 5:
Advanced Phone

Now that you have the basic phone features down, let's to explore the more advanced capabilities of the phone. In this chapter we will look at working with multiple callers and setting up Conference calling. We will also show you how to "Forward" your phone calls to another number. Lastly, we will show you how choose separate "Ringtones" for individual callers.

Call Waiting

Call waiting is built-in on the Pre™. If another call comes in while you are on the phone, just touch the "Green" phone button. The first call will be put on "hold" and you can answer the second call.

In the middle of the screen, below the first caller ID, there are two blue lines which is the "**Swap Caller**" button.

Touch the "**Swap Caller**" button and you can go to the previous call. When you "Swap Calls," the button then moves below the second caller.

NOTE: As of publishing time, there is **no** way to join these two calls into a "Conference Call." This may change with future releases of Palm Pre software.

Conference Calling

In today's busy world, working with several callers at once has become something that we demand from our Phones. Fortunately, conference calling is very intuitive on the Palm Pre.

Initiating the First Call

As we showed you in the previous chapter, make a call to any number – a contact, a new number – anyone.

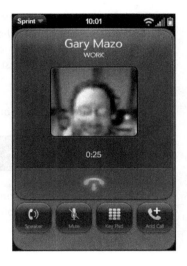

Move the Pre away from your face and you will see the phone "Menu" of options available to you. Most of these we covered in the last chapter.

Adding a Second Caller

Touch the "**Add Call**" button on the bottom left to add a second caller. This will immediately put the first caller on "Hold."

Touching the "**Add Call**" button will bring you to your main phone screen – you can search for the contact to add to this call, or you can just begin typing a name on the keyboard.

If the contact has more than one phone entry, you can just touch on the one you would like to call and the call will be initiated.

Merging Calls

Once the call to the second caller has been initiated, move the phone away from your face and you will notice that the "Merge Call" button has now been added under the first caller.

TIP: Press the red phone button to "End all calls"

TIP: To view a person's contact information you can simply tap their name on the phone screen.

Touch the "**Merge Calls**" button and both calls will be merged into a three-way "Conference Call."

The top of the screen will now show that you are in a "Conference" call.

Separating the Calls or To Talk Privately with someone in a Conference call

As of publishing time, In order to speak to one caller individually or privately from a conference call, until this is fixed with a software update, you will need to ask the other callers to simply hang up.

Call Forwarding

There may be times when you need to forward your calls to another number. Perhaps you are traveling to a friend's house and you want to forward calls to their "land line" because the cell reception at their house is poor.

Note: Depending on your wireless service provider, your phone may not have this feature.
Forwarded Calls May Cost Extra: Check with your wireless service provider about the pricing of forwarded calls; additional charges may apply for each forwarded call.

For Phones with the "Call Forwarding Feature"

Touch the "Phone" icon, tap the upper left corner to open the MENU, and tap **Preferences.**
In the **"Calls,"** section, set **Call Forwarding** to either **"On"** or **"Off."** Enter call forward number: Enter the number that you want to forward calls to. Tap to change an existing number.

For Phones without the "Call Forwarding Feature" (Notably on the Sprint Network)

If you do not see a "Call Forwarding" option in your Phone Preferences Menu, the following works (at least on Sprint at the time of publishing.)
Dial ***72NPANXXNNNN** (Area Code and Number) to start forwarding;
Dial ***720** to stop call forwarding.

Show or Block (Hide) Your Caller ID

You do not have the option with the Palm Pre to "Block" your caller ID at the time of the writing of this book. You can always dial *67 before any call to block the caller ID or call your wireless service provider and ask them if they will provide this service for all calls.

Ringtones, Sounds and Vibration

The Palm Pre can alert you to incoming calls, voice mails received and other features with unique sounds or vibrations. These can easily be adjusted using the "**Sounds and Ringtones**" Icon.

Changing the Default Ringtone

There is one Ringtone that the Palm Pre uses as the "Default" tone. This tone will be played for all calls that come in unless you give a contact a unique Ringtone which we will discuss further on in this chapter.

Go to your "**Sounds and Ringtones**" Icon and touch the Ringtone tab.

The default tone is listed as "Pre" next to Ringtone. Touch the tab and scroll through all the available Ringtones.

Each tone will play briefly if you touch the small, blue "**Play**" button on the right side.

When you find a tone you like, touch it to select it, then touch its name in the left side (gray area) to select it. You know it's selected when you see the checkmark next to the name – like "Older Phone" in the image.

Do the "Back" gesture to save your selection and return to the previous screen.
To adjust the volume of the Ringtone, slide the bar below the Ringtone switch.

Trying to preview a Ringtone and you cannot hear anything?

TIP: If you are trying to preview (listen to a Ringtone) and you hear nothing, check that your "Mute" Switch is OFF and your volume is not too low (see page 38.)

Using an MP3 File as the "Default Ringtone"

One cool feature of the Pre™ is the ability to use any MP3 file as a Ringtone.

Finding the MP3 to Use

Follow the procedure above to change a Ringtone.

You will notice that at the bottom left hand corner is a "soft key" with musical notes and a small **"+"** sign. Just touch

this icon.

All the MP3 files on your phone will now be shown to you. You can "Play" a preview, by touching the small "**Play**" button – or you can just select the song you wish to use.

Once selected, you will now see the name of the MP3 file listed next to "RINGTONE."

Adding "Vibration" to the Ring

The first switch in the "**Sounds and Ringtones**" icon deals with "Vibration." If you want the phone to Vibrate whenever you turn the "Ringer Switch" on the top of your phone to the "OFF" position, move this switch to the "ON" setting.

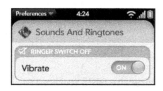

The second switch allows "**Vibration**" to be used even when the "Ringer Switch" is in the "On" position. Just move the switch to the "**ON**" or "**OFF**" position as you desire.

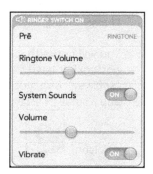

System Sounds

Under the "Ringtone Volume" slider in the same Icon is a switch marked "**System Sounds**." If you want other System sounds, for example the sound associated with closing a "Card," "Sending Email," or a "Calendar Reminder," this switch must be set to "**ON**." The default position is "**ON**."

You can adjust the volume of the "System Sounds" by simply moving the "Slider."

Assigning Unique Ringtones to Your Contacts

Sometimes, it is both fun and useful to give a unique Ringtone to a certain contact in your address book. This way, you know who is calling without looking at your phone.

For example, one of the authors (Gary) sets the Ringtone for his son Daniel to the Ringtone of Elton John's "Daniel." It is easy to know immediately when Daniel is calling.

Giving a Contact a Unique Ringtone

Open the "Contact" Icon – and search for the contact you want to change (in this case Daniel) by typing a few letters of the contact's first and/or last name.

Touch the "**Edit**" button 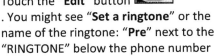 . You might see "**Set a ringtone**" or the name of the ringtone: "**Pre**" next to the "RINGTONE" below the phone number block.

We want to change that to Daniel's own unique Ringtone, so we touch the tab to see all the available tones.

If this contact has already been assigned a "Ringtone," we will be prompted with a message asking if we want to **"Change"** or **"Delete"** the Ringtone. In a case like this, we would choose **"Change."**

Now, we follow the same procedure as we did previously in searching for the MP3 file to use as a Ringtone.

Once we locate "Daniel," we touch it and it will show up as a new Ringtone in Daniel's profile.

Chapter 6:
Bluetooth

The Palm Pre ships with Bluetooth 2.0 Technology. Think of Bluetooth as a short range, wireless technology which allows your Palm Pre to "connect" to various peripheral devices without wires. Popular devices are headsets, computers, speaker systems, and vehicle sound systems.

Bluetooth Background

Bluetooth is believed to be named after a Danish Viking and King, Harald Blåtand (which has been translated as *Bluetooth* in English.) King Blåtand lived in the 10th century and is famous for uniting Denmark and Norway. Similarly, Bluetooth technology unites computers and telecom. His name, according to legend, is from his very dark hair, which was unusual for Vikings. Blåtand means dark complexion. There does exist a more popular story which states that the King loved to eat Blueberries, so much so his teeth became stained with the color Blue.

Sources:
http://cp.literature.agilent.com/litweb/pdf/5980-3032EN.pdf
http://www.cs.utk.edu/~dasgupta/bluetooth/history.htm
http://www.britannica.com/eb/topic-254809/Harald-I

Understanding Bluetooth

Bluetooth allows your Palm Pre to communicate with things like headsets, GPS devices and other hands-free systems with the freedom of wireless. Bluetooth is a small radio that transmits from each device. The Palm Pre gets "paired" – connected to the peripheral. Many Bluetooth devices can be used up to 30 feet away from the Palm Pre.

TIP: Learn more about what all the Bluetooth icons in the Status Bar mean on page 20.

Bluetooth Devices that work with the Palm Pre

The Palm Pre works with Bluetooth headsets, hands free car kits and Bluetooth Speakerphones. The Pre also supports **A2DP** – which is known as **"Stereo Bluetooth."**

With Stereo Bluetooth, you will be able to use your Palm Pre to play music using Bluetooth stereo headphones or a Bluetooth stereo system in your car or in your home.

Pairing with (Connecting to) a Bluetooth Headset

Your primary use for Bluetooth will most likely be with a Bluetooth headset for "Hands free" calling. Any Bluetooth headset should work well with your Palm Pre. To start using any Bluetooth device, you need to first "pair" it with your Palm Pre.

Turn "ON" Bluetooth

The first step to using Bluetooth is to turn the Bluetooth Radio "ON."

Tap the "**Launcher**" icon and swipe to the third screen and you should see the "**Bluetooth**" icon.

Touch the Bluetooth icon and move the slider to the "**ON**" position.

Once turned on, touch the "Add device" button so the Palm Pre will start searching for Bluetooth devices in range.

BATTERY SAVING TIP: Bluetooth is an added drain to your battery. If you don't plan on using Bluetooth for a period of time, think about turning the switch back to "**OFF**."

Pairing with a Headset or any Bluetooth Device

As soon as you turn Bluetooth "**ON**" and touch **"Add device**," the Palm Pre will begin to search for any nearby Bluetooth device – like a Bluetooth headset. Put your headset into "Pairing mode." Read the instructions carefully that came with your headset – usually there is a combination of buttons to push to achieve this.

TIP: Some headsets require you to press and hold a button for 5 seconds until you see quickly flashing blue, or red and blue, lights.

Once the Palm Pre detects the headset, it will attempt to "automatically" pair with the headset. If paring takes place automatically, there is nothing more for you to do.

 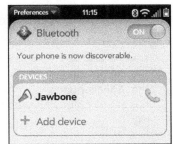

Notice the small blue icon – this tells you that this particular device is a Bluetooth Headset.

If the Palm Pre asks for a "PIN" or "Pass code" to be entered, the keyboard will be displayed and you enter the four digit pass code supplied by the headset manufacturer.

TIP: Most headsets use 0000 or 1234 which is why the Palm Pre can try to automatically pair with most headsets. Check your headset documentation to learn the correct pass code or PIN for your device.

Using the Bluetooth Headset

If your headset it properly "Paired" and "ON," all incoming calls should be routed to your headset. Usually you can simply press the main button on the headset to answer the call or use the "**Drag to Answer**" function on the Palm Pre.

Move the phone away from your face (while the Palm Pre is dialing) and you should see the indicator showing you that the Bluetooth headset is in use. In the image you see that the "**Bluetooth**" icon is in the "**Audio**" button.

You will also see the options to send the call to your Palm Pre handset or to the "Speaker phone." You can change this at any point while you are on the call.

Options when On a Call

Once the call is made and you are speaking with your contact, you can still re-route the call to either the Palm Pre or the Speakerphone.

Move the call away from your face (if it is near your face) and you will see

"**Audio**" icon  with the bluetooth symbol (as shown above) as one of the options for you to touch. Touch that icon and you will have all the options for re-routing the call to the headset (Normal) or the Speaker Phone (Speaker.)

You may choose to send the call to any of the options shown and you will see the small speaker icon move to the current source being used for the call.

Bluetooth Stereo

The Pre supports A2DP – known as Bluetooth Stereo – right out of the box. It is as easy to use a Bluetooth Stereo device as it is to use a Bluetooth Headset.

Pairing to a Bluetooth Stereo Device

Put your Bluetooth Stereo Device into "Pairing Mode" as you did above. In this illustration, we will use our Bluetooth Equipped Car Stereo.

We go through the pairing process as we did above and the Pre is able to detect that this device is capable of Streaming Bluetooth Stereo Music, so the icon changes from the "Headset" alone, to one with both "Musical Notes" (Stereo) and the "Headset."

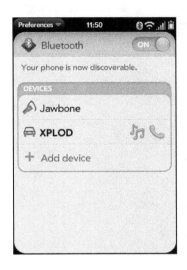

If your device is capable of both Bluetooth Stereo and being used as a Bluetooth Headset (as our unit is) both icons will be displayed.

TIP: We can then go to any Music source on the Pre – either the built in music player or services like Pandora Streaming Radio (see page 283) and the music will automatically come out the stereo system.

WHEN A PHONE CALL IS RECEIVED:
If a phone call comes in, the music will **automatically pause** and the Phone call will come through the Bluetooth Device (if it is Bluetooth Headset Compatible.) Once the call has ended, the music will simply resume where it left off.

Sending All Your Contacts to Your Car Bluetooth Kit

Once you connect your Pre to your car's Bluetooth stereo kit, you can send all your Pre's contacts to the car's contact list.

To do this, start your Contacts icon, tap the upper left corner to bring up the menu and select **"Send All to Car Kit"**

Chapter 7:
Using Wi-Fi

The Benefits of Wi-Fi

We live in a Wi-Fi world. Wireless Internet access
has become the rule, not the exception.
Sometimes, Wi-Fi networks sometimes provide
coverage where you cannot find it with your regular
cellular network - in a basement or in a building.

The beauty of the Pre is that it has built in Wireless Internet access. You
simply have to "Connect" your Pre to a wireless network and you can be
sending email and surfing the Web in minutes.

Do I need Wi-Fi to download some Apps and larger files?
Yes. Some larger Applications will require you to connect your Pre via Wi-
Fi to the web in order to install the App or large file you purchased.

Searching for a Network

The first thing to do is to go to locate
and tap your **"Wi-Fi"** App from your

Launcher.
Make sure that the Wi-Fi button is set
to "**ON.**"

Once Wi-Fi is "**ON,**" the Pre will
automatically begin to start looking for
Wireless networks.

The list of available Networks will be
shown under where it says: "**Choose a
Network**..." You can see in this screen
shot that we have just one network
"**Flint**" from which to choose.

NOTE: Palm actually recommends connecting to a Wi-Fi Network to save battery life. While that may seem a bit counter-intuitive – it really makes sense. Especially in a weak signal area, instead of searching for a high-speed cellular network data connection (which can really drain the battery), the Pre will perform most Data functions over Wi-Fi instead.

Connecting to a Network

In order to connect to any Network listed, simply touch it. If the network is unsecure (does not require a password), you will be connected automatically.

Secure Networks - Entering a Password

Some Networks require a password to "log-in." This is set when the network administrator originally created the wireless network. Make sure you have the exact password and know it is usually case sensitive so "Password" is not the same as "password."

If the network does require a password, you will be taken to the password entry screen. Type the password exactly as given to you and tap "Sign in" at the bottom of the screen. *TIP: Some conventions, offices, restaurants or other locations do require a password. If so, just ask someone in charge.*

Verifying Your Wi-Fi Connection

Touch the "**Wi-Fi**" icon on from your Launcher and you will be taken back to the "Settings" screen.

You should now see the name of your Wi-Fi network in the list with a Blue Check Mark showing that you are connected to this network.

Advanced Wi-Fi Options ("Hidden" or "Undiscoverable" Networks)

Why can't I see the Wi-Fi Network I want to join?

Sometimes, for security reasons, people make their networks "undiscoverable" and you will have to manually enter the name and security options to connect.

Tap the "+ Join network" at the bottom of the "Choose a Network" box:

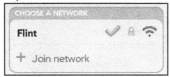

Make sure the cursor is in the **"Join Other Network"** field and type in the name of the Network (if it is not listed.)

Before you try to connect, ask the Network Administrator for help with the following:

- Name of the network
- Type of security used
- Passwords / Network Keys
- Any other settings required to connect

Type in the Wi-Fi Network Name and then touch the **"Security"** tab and choose which type of security is being used on that network.

Your choices are **"Open,"** **"WPA-personal,"** **"WEP"** or **"Enterprise,"** If you are unsure, you will need to acquire this information from the Network Administrator.

Then, type the password and this new network will be saved to your network list for future access. You should only have to enter this setup information once.

Network Specific Options (Troubleshooting)

If you are having trouble connecting to a specific network, or if the Network Administrator said you need to use advanced settings, you can change advanced settings for each network. Tap the name of the Network you are either connected to or wish to connect to.

Turn the switch for "**Automatic IP Settings**" to "**Off**" if it is "**On**."

NOTE: Only do this if you are having trouble connecting to the network and you or the Network Administrator knows the correct IP settings.

Manually add in the correct "**IP Address**," "**Subnet Address**," "**Gateway**" and/or "**DNS Server.**"

Touch "**Done**" and then perform the "Back Gesture" and see if you are connected to the network.

Forget (or Erase) a Network

If you find that you no longer want to connect to a network on your list you can "**forget**" it – essentially take it off your list of networks. Tap the "Network Name" as you did above and go to the "Network Details Screen."

Scroll all the way to the bottom of the Network Settings screen.
Touch "**Forget this Network**" at the bottom of the screen.
NOTE: As of publishing time, you are not prompted with any warning to confirm that you want to Forget the network, so be careful. You will be disconnected from the Network.

Chapter 8:
Contacts

The Palm Pre is built from the ground up to synchronize with your contacts (and calendar) wirelessly and automatically. For this to work you need to be using Google Contacts/Calendar, Facebook, LinkedIn, Microsoft Exchange or any other service currently supported by Synergy. Other options (types of accounts) will likely be added in the future. We show you other syncing options as well if you do not use any of the above applications or web services.

Importing Contacts from Other Programs

On Page 54, we discussed setting up your Pre for the first time syncing your contacts.

We discussed using Google Contacts on Page 70 which offers true "Cloud Synchronization" of your data in real time.

You can also sync with standalone desktop software, but you will need to acquire Third Party software to enable this 'desktop sync.' Once your contacts are set up for syncing with your Pre, they will update each time you connect your Pre to your PC or Mac. (See page 60)

Other Ways to Add New Contacts

TIP: You can add new Contact entries from Email Messages you receive. Learn how on page 142.

TIP: You can add new contacts from phone calls you have placed or your call logs. Learn how on page 108.

Synergy™

If you have not already reviewed it, take a few minutes to check out our Synergy™ overview on page 57. You will have a good understand of all the various options to sync contacts (and calendar) to your Pre.

Adding New Account to Sync with Contacts

To add your Google®, facebook®, Exchange™ or other account, just start your "Contacts" App. The "Contacts" icon is, by default, located in the Quick Launch Bar.

Touch the "**Contacts**" tab in the upper left hand corner and then touch "**Preferences and Account**."

Your current accounts are listed. Touch the "Add Account" button to add a new Account to your profile. Just choose whether you want to add a "Google,® facebook,® LinkedIn, or Exchange™ account and input your login information – that's all there is to it.

NOTE: You are likely to see even more Account types in the future. LinkedIn was recently added and we hear rumors that Yahoo will be added soon.

Once you tap an Account button, then you will be prompted to enter your login username and password.

Finally, after successfully logging into this new account, you will see all your contacts from this account 'flow' automatically into your Palm Pre and be linked to the correct contacts already in your Contact List.

Notice that the LinkedIn profile for Martin was automatically linked with all his other profiles.

Setting your "Default" Account

Once you have more than one account for your contacts, you will need to specify which is the "default" account. Here we have selected Google as our Default.

This default account is used when you add new contacts to your Pre.

Adding a New Contact

You always have the option of adding your contacts right on your Pre. You might find yourself away from your computer, but carrying your Pre and you need to add someone to your "Contacts" – this is very easy to do.

Start the Contacts Icon

From your Home Screen, tap the "**Contacts**" icon and you will see your Contact list. Just touch the small "+" sign in the lower left hand corner to add a new contact.

Touch the "**Name**" button and input the new contact's first and last name. You may also add a "**Company**" as well on the next line.

Adding a New Phone Number

Touch the "**New Phone Number**" button and type in the phone number.

TIP: Don't worry about parentheses, dashes or dots, the Pre will put the number into the correct format – just type the digits of the area code and number.

Touch the small box that indicates the "type" of phone number and select whether this is a "**Mobile**," "**Home**," "**Work**," "**Fax**" or "**Other**" number.

Adding "Pauses" (Dialing Extensions and More)

Sometimes you might need to have an extension or additional code after one or more of your numbers. Adding a "Pause" in the dial string will do just that. To add a "Pause" press the "**p**" key. The "Pause" will be displayed as a "comma." When the phone number is dialed, the comma will turn into a 2-second pause.

TIP: for more of a "soft pause" use the letter "t" instead of the letter "p."

Changing the Default Ringtone for a Contact

Tap the "**Set a Ringtone**" tab under the phone number to change the default ringtone for a contact. The Ringtone options included the built in ringtones on the Pre as well as any ringtones you might create from your own music collection –see page 119.

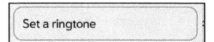

Just touch a new Ringtone to change the Ringtone for the contact – you can always preview the Ringtone by touching the "**Play**" button.

Once you choose a new Ringtone, just use the "Back" Gesture and you will see the new Ringtone listed under the contact information.

Using your Own Music for a Ringtone

Touch the Ringtone tab as you did above and then touch the icon in the lower left hand corner.

Browse your music collection and choose any song – in this case, we chose "Cheeseburger in Paradise" for Martin's ringtone.

Once we choose the song, the Pre will make a Ringtone of that song and place it in the Ringtones list. We scroll the list and choose "Cheeseburger in Paradise" for Martin's ringtone.

Adding Email Address and Web Site

Touch the "**New Email Address**" tab and input the Email Address for your contact. You can also touch the tab under the email address and select whether this is a home, work or other email address.

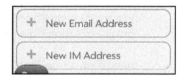

You can then add a "**New IM Address**" using the same procedure.

Under the "**New URL**" tab you will also see places to add additional Reminders, Birthday, Spouse, Children or Nickname. You might also see a line that says PIN. If you are a BlackBerry user and have synced your contacts from either Outlook or Entourage or Mac Mail you might see the PIN line available. A PIN is a unique identifying number for BlackBerry devices.

To add the Website of your Contact, just touch "**Add new URL**" and input the web site.

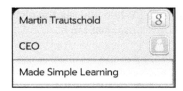

Adding the Address

Under the URL tab is the tab for adding the address. Input the Street, City, State and Zip Code. You can also specify the Country and whether this is a home or work address.

When you are done, perform a "Back" gesture.

Adding a Photo to Contacts (Picture Caller ID and More)

From the "**Add new Contact**" screen we have been working in, just touch the "**Add Photo**" box next to the "**Name**" tab.

You then have the option to use a "**New Photo**" (which will launch the Camera) or simply choose one of the photos on your Pre.

Tap the Photo Album in which the picture is located.

When you see the picture you want to use, just tap it.

Adjust and Center the Picture:
You will notice that the top and bottom become "grayed out" and that the picture can be manipulated by moving it, pinching to "Zoom in" or "Zoom out" and then arranged in the picture window.

Once the Picture is sitting where you want it, touch "**Attach Photo**" and that picture will be set for the Contact.

Searching Your Contacts

Let's say you need to find a specific phone number or email address. Just start your "**Contacts**" App as we did above. Type a name on your keyboard – first letter, complete name – just type a search term and the Contacts will move to find your contact.

Input the first few letters of any of these three searchable fields:

- First Name
- Last Name
- Company Name

The Pre will begin to 'filter' and display only those contacts that match the letters typed.

TIP: To further narrow the search, hit the "space" key and type a few more letters.

When you see the correct name, just touch the name and that individuals contact information will appear.

How can I get the Company Name to be displayed in my Contact List?
When you type a few letters of a company name, you will see all matching entries. However, you will not see the company name unless you have selected to show "**Company**" in your "**List Order**" inside your Contact "**Preferences & Accounts**" screen.

Search by "Flicking"

If you don't want to manually input letters, you can just move your finger and "Flick" from the bottom up and you will see your Contacts move quickly on the screen. Just continue to Flick or Scroll until you see the name you are looking for. Just touch the name and the contact information will appear.

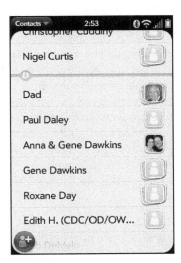

Adding Contacts from Emails

Often times, you might receive an Email and realize that the contact is not in your Address book. Adding a new "Contact" from an email is easy.

Open the Email from the Contact you wish to add to your Contact list. In the **"From"** field of the Email, just touch the name of the "Sender" next to the "From:" tag.

If the "Sender" is not already in your address book, you will be taken to a screen that will ask you whether you want to add that Email and "Name" to your "Contacts."

If you select **"Add to Contacts"** you will be taken to a new screen.

Choose "Save as New" if this is a new contact.

If you would like to add this Email address to an existing contact. For example, if this is someone's personal email address and you already have an entry with their work email, then you would select **"Add to Existing "** and choose the correct person. Then, you will have to give this email address a tag, like 'work' or 'personal.'

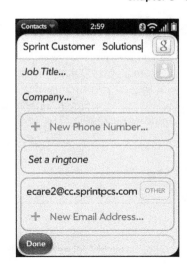

If you select "**Save as New**" you will notice that the "Name" and "Email" will be filled in for you. Just add any other pertinent information. When you are done, just touch the "**Done**" button at the bottom.

Sending a Picture to a Contact

If you want to send a picture to a contact, you will need to do that from either the Camera Icon (see page 228) or from the Photos Icon (see page 239).

Sending an Email Message from Contacts

Since many of the core Icons (Contacts, Phone, Mail and Messages) are fully integrated, one Icon can easily trigger another. So, if you want to send an Email to one of your Contacts, simply tap the contact's email address and your Mail App will launch so you can compose and send the message.

Start your "Contacts" by touching the "**Contacts**" icon. Either "Search" or "Flick" through your contacts until you find the contact for which you are searching. (See page 140 for Contact searching tips.)

In the contact information, touch the email address of the Contact you would like to use.

You will see that the "Mail" program launched automatically with the Contact's name in the "To" field of the Email. Type and send the message.

Mapping Your Contacts (Google Maps)

One of the very cool things about the Pre is the integration with Google Maps. This is very evident in the Contacts Icon. Let's say you want to map a home or work address of any contact in your address book.

In the old days (pre-Pre) you would have to use "Google" or use "MapQuest" or some other program and laboriously re-type the address information. Very time consuming -- Not so on the Pre.

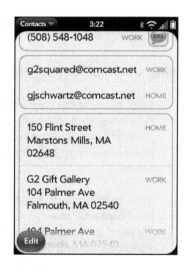

Simply open the Contact as you did above. This time, touch the "Address" at the bottom of the Contact information.

Immediately, your Google Maps will load and drop a red indicator "push pin" at the exact location of the Contact.

The Address or Name of Location will appear in a tab at the top.

Touch the "**Results**" button to get more information.

Now you may select "**Directions To Here**" or "**Directions From Here.**"

Then, type the correct start or end address and touch the "**Route**" button in the lower right hand corner. If you decide you don't want the directions, just tap the "**Clear**" button in the top left.

Tap "**Menu**" in the lower right corner to see this menu:

TIP: To return to your "Contact" information, just "Swipe up" reducing Google Maps to a "Card" and swipe through your cards to your "Contacts," which were automatically reduced to a "Card" when Google Maps launched.

Using Contact Reminders

Have you ever been on the phone with someone and as soon as you hung up the phone say: "Oh, I meant to ask him/her about....." Well, the Pre has anticipated that and included a great feature called "Contact Reminders."

Setting up the Reminder

In each Contact entry, there is a box entitled "**Reminder**." Just choose to "**Edit**" the contact and then touch the box and input a reminder for that particular contact entry.

You can also touch the "Contact" tab at the top of any contact entry and just select "**Add Contact Reminder**" from the Menu.

NOTE: The reminder remains active until you remove it at a later date.

How "Reminders" Work

Once the "Reminder" is set, each time that particular "Contact" either calls, emails or sends you an SMS, MMS or other "Message" – or each time you call him/her or send a message to that "Contact, " a "Reminder" will appear at the bottom of the screen.

The "Reminder" is just like other "Notifications" – it appears small and

innocuously at the bottom of the screen ![icon] – touch it once and you can read the reminder at the bottom – touch it again and you will be taken to the "Contact Reminder" section of that particular "Contact" entry.

Adding a Contact to Your Launcher ("Add To Launcher")

There is a great way on the Pre to add your favorite contacts to the Launcher – this puts their face right on your Launcher screen. (Unless you don't have a picture for them, then you just see their name.)

To add someone to the Launcher, open your Contacts list, select the contact and bring up the menu. From the menu select "**Add To Launcher**," then you have the chance to change how their name is displayed on their icon. You can change the Icon's name or add a nickname by typing a new name in the fields.

This allows you to more easily and quickly stay in touch with them. Once you add someone to the launcher, just 'ride the wave' to quickly get to them – you can Instant Message, Call, Email assuming you have all their information on your Pre.

Changing Contact Display and Sort Order – "List Order"

From the screen above, touch the drop down menu under "List Order." You can have your contacts listed by either "First Name," "Last Name," "Company & First Name" or "Company & Last Name."

Contact Troubleshooting

Sometimes, your Contacts Icon might not work the way you are hoping. If you don't see all your contacts, review the steps for Syncing Contact information on page 63

Sometimes, you might change your Contacts information on your computer, but you don't see the information on your Pre. You might just need to "Manually Sync" your contacts.

From the Contacts App, just touch the "**Contacts**" tab and then touch "**Sync Now**" to get both computer and Pre in Sync.

Chapter 9:
Calendar

Manage your Busy Life on your Pre

The "Calendar" App is a powerful and easy to use application that really helps you manage your appointments, keep track of what you have to do, set reminder alarms and even accept Meeting Initiations (for Enterprise users).

Today's Day and Date Shown on Calendar Icon

The Calendar Icon is usually right on your Pre Home Screen in the Quick Launch Bar. You will quickly see that your Calendar Icon changes to show today's date and day of the week. The icon to the right shows that it is the 8th of the month.

Syncing or Sharing Your Calendar(s) with your Pre

If you use Google Calendar, Facebook, you can synchronize or share that calendar with your Pre by setting up an automatic wireless synchronization (see page 70). We really recommend that you use either the Google Calendar option or a Microsoft Exchange Server (if you have one) or, even both – that's the cool thing about the Pre!

If you use a desktop application and do not use Google Calendar or have access to a Microsoft Exchange server at work, then there are other options to allow you to sync your calendar. See page 59 for Desktop Sync options.

After you setup the calendar sync, all of your computer calendar appointments will be synced into your Pre calendar automatically based on your Sync settings. If you use a third party solution to sync with your calendar (e.g. Microsoft Outlook, Entourage or Apple's iCal), your appointments will be transferred or synced every time you connect your Pre to your computer.

If you use another method to sync (e.g. Exchange, Google Sync, or similar) this sync is wireless and automatic and will most likely happen without you having to do anything after the initial setup process.

Setting up a Google Calendar

See page 70 for help getting started with Google Calendar and Contacts.

Setting up Your Facebook Calendar

As of publishing time, the Pre only synced with the main Facebook "Event Calendar," not any of the over 300 other calendar apps available in Facebook.

The main "Event Calendar" is designed to be used for scheduling events like parties, training session, group get togethers. This calendar is not meant to be a true 'personal calendar.'

What is synced from the Facebook calendar?

If you schedule a new event on the Facebook Event Calendar or reply "RSVP" to an event, then those items will show up on your Pre. NOTE: If you do not RSVP to an event to which you are invited, this event will not appear on your Pre calendar.

How quickly will events sync?

This calendar sync is wireless and automatic and will most likely happen every 15 minutes without you noticing it.
TIP: Like with Contacts, you can 'force a sync' by going into the "Preferences & Accounts" screen and scrolling to the bottom where you press "Sync Now."

Viewing your Schedule and Getting Around

The default view for the Calendar is your "Day" view. It will show you at a glance any upcoming appointments for your day. Appointments are shown in your calendar. If you happen to have several different calendars, like "Work" and "Home" on your computer or "Google" and "Facebook," you will see these as separate colors on your Pre calendar.

Events created in your "Google" Calendar will be a different color than those created in your "Exchange" or "Outlook" calendar as well.

MOVE DAY AT A TIME:
Swipe left or right to look at the next day or the previous day on the calendar.

CHANGING VIEWS:
Use the **"Day," "Week,"** and **"Month"** buttons at the bottom.

JUMP TO TODAY:
Touch the "**Day**" view button to jump to Today's date in day view.

Adding Weather Forecast to Your Google and Pre Calendar

Inside Google Calendar, you can add your local weather forecast to show up as an all-day event on your Pre. To add weather to your Google calendar, click the "Settings" link at the top of Google Calendar.

Sync | 🔽 | Settings | Help | Sign out

Then scroll down to near the bottom to enter your location (e.g. City name or Postal/ Zip Code). Then, in "Show my weather based on Location", check the °C or °F so the weather shows up in the correct units.

Free Tips and Video Tutorials at www.MadeSimpleLearning.com

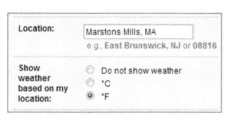

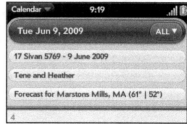

Make sure to "Save" your settings. Now you will have your local weather show up as a small bar across the top of each day in your Pre Calendar.

TIP: If the weather does not show up right away on your Pre, then try going to "Preferences & Accounts" from the menu. Scroll down and press the "Sync Now" button at the bottom.

TIP: If you still don't see the weather, then power down your Pre completely and turn it back on. This should force the Pre to re-sync all calendars and you should now see your weather.

Calendar Day, Week and Month Views

Your Pre Calendar comes with three views: Day, Week and Month as shown below. You can switch views by tapping the name of the view at the bottom of the screen.

DAY VIEW:

When you start your calendar, the default view is usually the "Day" view. The "Top" of the "Day View" shows "All Day Events. The main body of the day view shows scheduled appointments for the day.

This allows you to quickly see everything you have scheduled for the day. At the bottom of the calendar are buttons to change the view.

WEEK VIEW:

Touch the "**Week**" view button at the bottom and you can see a layout of appointments and events for the coming week. Colored "boxes" in the midst of a particular date indicate upcoming appointments and events.

To Move to a new week – just "Swipe" left or right.

To view an Event or day – tap your finger on that event or day.

MONTH VIEW:

Touch the "**Month**" view button at the bottom to see a layout of the full month. Days with appointments have grayed out squares in them. The gray squares roughly are positioned with your appointments – in other words, a square at the top of the day means an earlier appointment.

The current day will show up highlighted with a blue circle around it.

GO TO NEXT MONTH: Swipe "Up" once

GO TO PREVIOUS MONTH: Swipe "Down" once

To look on another day while in Month view, just touch a different date.

To return to "Today" just touch the "**Today**" tab at the bottom left.

Working with Several Calendars (Different Colors)

Your Pre Calendar can keep various calendars. The number of calendars you see depends on how you setup your synchronization using Google Calendar or other sync methods

In the appointments in my calendar, we have our "Google" calendar appointments showing up in Green and our "Palm Profile" appointments in Blue. The Weather Calendar is Yellow and US Holidays are in Red. Take a look back on Page 99 for more information.

HOW TO CHANGE THE COLORS?
Go to Preferences and Accounts and touch the Account you wish to change.

VIEWING ONLY ONE CALENDAR:
To view just one calendar at a
time, tap the "All" button
at the top and select only the
calendar you wish to see.

Touch the box with the color and then choose any other color from the menu.

Adding a New Calendar to your Pre

It's a 2-Step process to add a new calendar to sync with your Pre:

Step 1: First, if you don't already have the calendar setup on your computer, you need to set it up from your computer. In order to do the easiest sync from your new calendar to the Pre, we recommend you setup a new Google Calendar, Facebook calendar, or Outlook Calendar that is linked to a Microsoft Exchange server.

If you already have, or choose to setup, a calendar that only resides on your computer 'a stand-alone calendar' (e.g. Outlook not connected to a server, Sage ACT!, or iCal), then you will need to acquire Third Party software to allow you to sync with your Pre. See page 60 for help. Most of these Third Party solutions end up syncing from your 'stand alone' computer calendar to a Google Calendar. Then, the Pre takes care of the sync between Google and your Pre. In these instances, select "Google" in Step 2 to complete the sync.

Step 2: Inside your Pre calendar, bring up the menu by tapping or swiping down on the 'Calendar' menu in the upper left corner. Tap on the **"Preferences & Accounts"** menu item.

Scroll down to **"Add Account"** at the bottom to see the screen shown.

Tap the correct account type "Google," "Facebook" or "Microsoft Exchange" and enter your username and password to log into to your calendar account.

Adding New Calendar Appointments / Events

You can easily add new appointments right on your Pre and they will be synced (or shared with) your computer the next time the sync takes place.

All new appointments are added to the DEFAULT calendar as set in your "Preferences & Accounts" screen inside the Calendar App.

Adding a New Appointment

"Touch" the screen at a particular time to set an appointment; The **"New Event"** window will be displayed.

Quick Entry
Tap the time block in Day View and start typing your event for a "Quick Entry."

Detailed Entry

Touch the small "i"  on the right side to view the detailed event scheduling screen.

Type in a "Name" for the event. Make sure that the "Event" is going into the correct calendar – here it is going into our "Google" calendar.

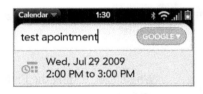

To change the calendar, tap the Calendar name in the upper right corner "Google" and select a different calendar.

Next, touch the "Date and Time" box. Touch each box to set the correct Date, Start Time and End Time.

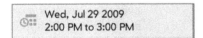

Touch the Starts / Ends tab to adjust the event timing.

TO CHANGE THE START TIME:
Touch the "**Date and or time**" field in the Month, Date and Year Boxes to choose the correct date and day. Then, scroll through the fields to reflect the correct date and start time of the appointment.

TO CHANGE THE END TIME:
Touch "**Date and or Time**" field and use the rotating dials.

TO SET AN ALL-DAY EVENT:

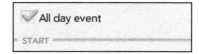

Touch the box next to "**All day event**" to make this an 'all day event.'

When done setting the timing, use the "Back" gesture, a quick right to left swipe in the Gesture Area to save your settings.

Recurring Events (Repeat Events)

Some of your appointments happen every day, week or month at the same time. If the appointment you are scheduling is a repeating or 'recurring' appointment, touch the "**Repeat**" tab and then select the correct option from the list.

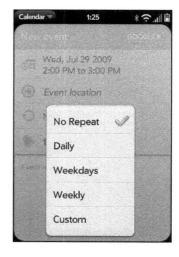

Swipe "Back" in the Gesture area and the event will reflect the new changes.

DAILY REPEATING:
Choose "Daily" if you want to repeat every day, or every few days – set the number of days between repeating on the screen as shown.

Tap the number to adjust the number of days between repeating.

You can then select the "REPEAT UNITL" as "Forever" by checking the box or until a specific date. Notice the 'plain text' description of the repeating interval at the bottom of the screen.

WEEKLY REPEATING:
If you have an event that repeats every week (or some number of weeks), then tap "Weekly."

Notice that you can check or uncheck the specific days of the week.

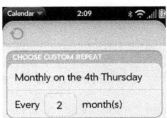

MONTHLY REPEATING:
You have a couple of options for Monthly repeating.

You can set the even to occur on a specific "4th Thursday" or "1st Monday" or you may choose to repeat the event on exactly the same date of the month – e.g. the 24th of the month.

Swipe "Back" to save your changes.

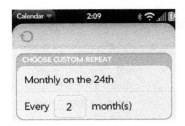

ANNUAL / YEARLY RECURRING:
Choose Yearly recurring for events like Birthdays and Anniversaries

which repeat every year.

TIP: You can also put Birthdays in the Contacts Icon. Each person has a "BIRTHDAY" field near the bottom of their contact entry.

Adding Alerts (Alarms) to Calendar Events

Alerts can be useful – an audible and visible reminder of an upcoming appointment can certainly keep you from forgetting an important event.

Touch the "**Alert**" tab (the picture of the Bell) and then select the option for a reminder alarm. You can have no alarm at all or set a time from 5 minutes before all the way to 1 day before – whatever works best for you. TIP: You can change the default alert time. See page 169.

Swipe "Back" to save your changes.

Choosing Which Calendar to Use

Let's say you keep a "Google," "Exchange," and a "facebook" calendar and you sync your Pre with all of them. You might need to decide that you want to schedule an appointment for just one of them.

Touch the "Active Calendar" tab to see all your calendars. Tap the calendar you want to use for this particular event. Usually, the calendar selected is the last one you selected for the previous event you scheduled on your Pre.

I scheduled a new event on the wrong calendar, how can I switch it?

In the example to the right, we scheduled a "Test Appointment" in our "Google" Calendar and we want to reschedule it in our "Palm Profile" calendar.

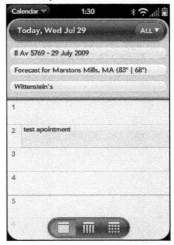

Initially, the appointment is in "Green" and it says "Google" in the upper right hand corner.

We touch "Palm Profile"

and the appointment now turns "Blue" in the entry screen and in the calendar itself.

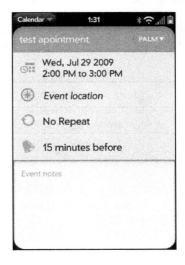

Adding Notes to Calendar Events

If you want to add some notes to this calendar event, tap "Event Notes" and type a few notes.

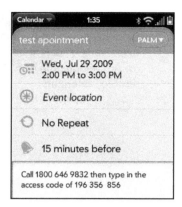

TIP: If this is a scheduled conference call or call with someone, just type their phone number in the Notes field.

Using the "Event Location" feature in the Calendar App

As long as you put in a location that is recognizable to Google Maps, you can show the location of a calendar event and even get directions to it.

First, you need to add a location to the Calendar event. Open up the Calendar scheduling input screen and add the location of the meeting or event in the "Event Location" line.

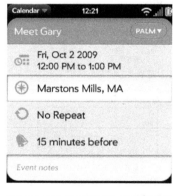

TIP: Enter as much information as you have in this field – Town, State and even the full address.

Once the Event Location is entered, when the alarm reminder rings, tap the event to open it. Then you can Map the event using Google Maps.

Mapping or Getting Directions to the Event Location

In your Calendar App, open up the Calendar appointment by touching it, then touch the "Calendar" MENU in the top left hand corner.

Touch the "Event Location" tab and you will see two options: "Show on Map" and "Get Directions."

Both options will load your Google Maps App.

To show the meeting or Event Location on the map, tap "Map Location."

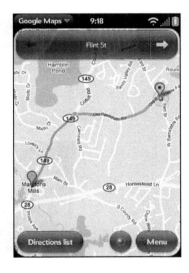

To get directions in Google Maps, touch the "Get Directions" tab and Google maps will calculate a route to the Event with step-by-step directions shown at the top. See page 288 for more information on directions in Google Maps.

Editing Appointments

Sometimes, the details of an appointment may change and need to be adjusted. Fortunately, this is an easy task on your Pre.

First, locate the appointment that needs to change and touch it. Just touch any Field you wish to edit in exactly the same manner in which you initially input the information.

Just touch the tab in the field you need to adjust. So, for example, to change the time of this appointment, touch the "**Date/Time**" tab and adjust the time for either the start or end times.

Deleting a Calendar Appointment

In your Calendar App (maximize the Card if you are in "Card View) Hold the "Orange" key and touch an appointment in your Calendar. You will be prompted to "Delete" the appointment. Either confirm the "Delete" or "Cancel."

NOTE: As you would expect, deleting an event from your Pre that is linked to another calendar such as Google or Microsoft Exchange will also delete that same calendar event off of the linked calendar.

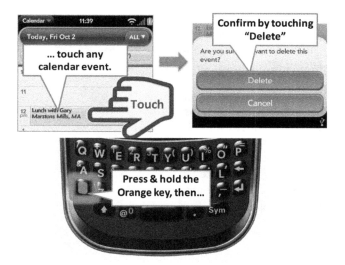

You can also delete the event from the Menu.

Touch the "**Calendar**" tab in the upper left corner to bring up the menu from the event details screen and then touch "Delete Event."

Touch "**Delete**" in the confirmation window and the event will be deleted.

Moving Events or Dragging & Dropping Them

In Day View on your calendar, if you need to change the time of a meeting (and it is still on the same day), the easiest way to do it is to drag and drop it.

In day view, you need to tap and hold your finger on the calendar event until it turns dark ('selected').

Then while still touching the screen, drag your finger up or down in the calendar to move the appointment. Let go when you have the appointment at the new time.

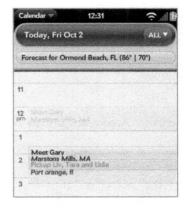

You will then see the event be placed on the calendar where you dropped it.

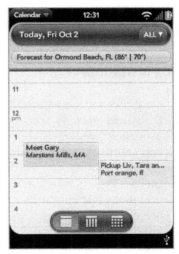

Free Time

The Pre uses a nice 'accordion' view of showing "Free Time" on your calendar – this allows you to see as many appointments as possible on the small screen.

Accordion View

Free time is displayed in an "Accordion Style" on the Pre calendar. To save space and let you see more of your daily schedule – Free time is condensed. In the midst of the "Accordion" you can see how many hours of your day are free.

Expanding the "Accordion" of Free Time

To show you day in an "Expanded" view – just touch the "Accordion" and the time will expand to show all the hours that can now still be filled up with appointments

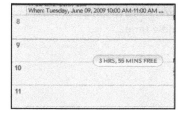

Meeting Invitations

For those who use Microsoft Exchange with Outlook, Google Calendar or Entourage regularly, meeting invitations become a way of life. You receive a meeting invitation in your email, you accept the invitation and then the appointment is automatically inserted into your calendar.

On your Pre, you will see that invitations that you "Accept" on your PC or Mac get inserted right into your calendar. Unfortunately, as of publishing time there is no way to actually "Accept" a meeting invitation on your Pre itself. (Although we are told they are working on this)

If you touch on the Meeting Invitation in your calendar you can see all the details that you need – the dial in number, meeting ID or any other details that might be in the invitation.

NOTE: As of publishing time, you could not "create" a meeting invitation on the Pre – this needs to be done via your desktop calendar application.

When you do accept it via your desktop application, like your "Google" calendar, you will get a reminder on your Pre like any other appointment.

Calendar Options

There are just a few options to adjust in your Calendar.

To adjust options, bring up the menu by touching the "**Calendar**" tab in the upper left hand corner. Then select "**Preferences & Accounts**."

The first option is the ability to change the "First Day of the Week" in the Calendar. The Default is "Sunday."

Touch the Day listed and choose any other day you wish to use as the "Beginning" of the week in Week View.

Next, you can choose the "Default Start and End" times for a typical day. The Default of 9 and 5 are set for you. You will want to change these to earlier and later if you have Breakfast or Dinner meetings.

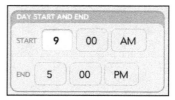

Changing Default Event Reminders (Alerts)

The Pre will set reminders at 15 Minutes Before the event unless you change this setting. You can always edit the details for each individual appointment as we showed you on Page 162.

Just touch the tab and choose a new setting to change the "Default" setting, which will be applied to all calendar appointments unless edited.

Play Sound for Event Reminders

Event reminders show up as notifications on the bottom of the screen as shown. You also have the option to have Event Reminders "Play a Sound." This can be helpful – but also a bit distracting. NOTE: If you are in a meeting or a meal and forget to set the Pre set to "Vibrate" this can be disruptive.

To Play a sound (as of publishing time there was no way to change the Tone used by the Pre) move this switch to the "On" position.

Change Default Event Duration

The Default Event Duration is set for 1 Hour, but you can change that by touching this tab and choosing 30 Minutes, 1 Hour or 2 Hours.

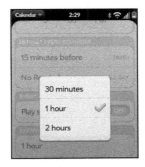

Changing the Default Calendar for New Events

We mentioned earlier that you can have multiple calendars displayed on your Pre. This option allows you to choose which Account will be your "Default" calendar.

That means that when you go to schedule every new appointment, this calendar will be selected by default.

If you wish to use a different calendar – say, your "Palm Profile" calendar, you can just change that when you actually set the appointment as shown on page 160

Sync Now - Forcing a Sync with Your Other Calendars

If you use "Google Calendar," "Exchange" or "facebook," your calendar changes are automatically synced with "Cloud Synchronization" about every 15 minutes.

Sometimes, you might make a change in one and it is not reflected in the other. If this happens, touch the "Sync Now" button to force a Synchronization between the calendars.

Chapter 10:
Email

Your Pre for "Anywhere, Anytime" Access to Email

Mobile email is certainly all the rage today. Depending on your wireless carrier (phone company) you will typically have unlimited email Included in your Pre data plan. With the Pre, mobile email is available via your wireless (cellular) signal and your Wi-Fi connection. (For help with Wi-Fi, see page 130.)

Setting up Email on the Pre

Touch your "**Mail**" icon – usually in the Quick Launch Bar. The first time the Email App loads, you should see the "**Add An Account**" button.

If you already have an email account set up – bring up the menu by tapping or swiping down in the upper left corner where it says "**Email.**"

From the drop down menu, choose "**Preferences & Account**s."

Adding a New Email Account from "Preferences & Accounts"

To add a new email account from the "**Preferences & Accounts**" menu, tap "**Add An Account**" below your email accounts. If you have no accounts set up, you will only see the "**Add An Account**" option.

TIP: To Edit any Email account, touch that account.

Input your Email address and Password in the boxes provided for you.

Just touch "Sign in" and you will be taken to the next screen – either you account will be set up automatically or you will have to specify information about your particular account.

Specifying Incoming and Outgoing Servers

Similar to setting up an email account on your computer, sometimes you will need to manually input the settings of your particular account.

You will have to put in the incoming mail server address, the user name and the password. If you don't know these settings, contact your ISP (Internet Service Provider) and they will be able to provide them for you. Usually, your incoming mail server is something like mail.nameofyourisp.com.

Once your input the information for your incoming server, you will now need to specify the information for your outgoing server.

In the outgoing server information, you put in the outgoing server address – usually either **smtp.nameofyourisp.com** or **mail.nameofyourisp.com**.

You can try to leave the name and password blank – if it doesn't work, you can go back and change it.

You may be asked if you want to use SSL (secure socket layer) – a type of outgoing mail security that may be required by your ISP. If you don't know whether you need it or not, just check the mail settings with your ISP.

Verifying that Your Account is Set Up

Once all the information is entered, the Pre will attempt to configure your email account.

You may receive an error message – in which case you need to review the information and try again. Usually, this is because the password has been mis-typed.

If you are taken to the screen that shows all your email accounts, look for the new account name. If you see it, your account was set up correctly.

Getting Started With Mail

To launch the Email App, tap the "Mail" icon on your home screen. The first screen you will see is the list of your accounts. The Pre will begin to check for new mail and then display the number of new messages for each account.

Composing a New Email Message

When you start the "Mail" App, your first screen should be your "Accounts" screen.

At the bottom left hand corner of the screen, you will see the "Compose" icon.

Tap the "**Compose**" icon to get started creating a new message.

Addressing Your Message - Choose the Recipients

Then, you need to address your message, you have several options depending on whether or not the person is in your Contact List

Option 1: Type an email address - notice the "@" and "." keys on the bottom to help you typing.

Option 2: Type a few letters of someone's first name; assuming you have them in your address book, the person's name should appear on the list, tap to select their name.

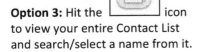

Option 3: Hit the [icon] icon to view your entire Contact List and search/select a name from it.

DELETING A RECIPIENT:

If you need to delete a name from the recipient list (To:, Cc: or Bcc:), tap the name to highlight it and then hit the backspace key.

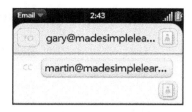

TIP: If you want to delete the last recipient you typed (and the cursor is sitting next to that name), just hit the delete key once to select the name and again to delete it.

Choose which Email Account to Send From

If you have more than one Email account set up, the Pre will use whichever account you designated as the "Default" account. If you want to specify an account to have as the sending account for this email, just touch the "From" line and all your Email Accounts will be displayed at the bottom. Just choose the "sending" account from the list.

Type in a Subject

Touch the "**Subject**" line and enter in text for the subject of the email and press the Enter key or tap in the "Body" area of the email.

Type Your Message

Now that the cursor is in your "Body" section (under the subject line), you can start typing your email message.

EMAIL SIGNATURES: If you have set up an Email Signature for the account you are using, it will be displayed at the bottom of the body of the email message. See page 186 to learn how to change your email signature.

Send your Email

Once you have typed your message and proof read the text, simply touch the "Send" (paper airplane) in the lower right hand corner.

Your Email will be sent and you should hear the "sent" sound that is played on the Pre, (unless you have this set not to play a sound – see page 121) confirming that your mail was sent. You should see a notification at the bottom of the screen, too:

Checking Sent Messages

To Confirm that the Email was sent, go to the Account folder of the account you just used to send the last message. You should see an "**Inbox**," a "**Sent**" folder and a "**Trash**" folder.

Go into the Sent folder and you should see the latest email that was just "Sent."

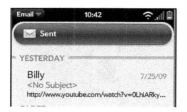

NOTE: You will only see the "Sent" and "Trash" folders if you have actually sent or deleted email from that account on the Pre. If your Email account is an IMAP account, you will see many folders other than those listed above.

Reading and Replying to Mail

Touch one of the mail tabs and you will see your email for that particular email account.

The first screen shows your inbox, outbox and trash for that particular account.

To read your messages, touch your "**Inbox**." New, unread messages are shown with a small blue dot to the left of the message – just like in the Mail program on Mac Computers.

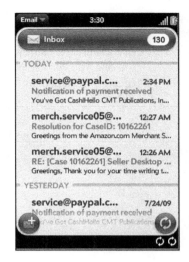

You can scroll through your messages by moving your finger and flicking through the messages. When you want to read a message, simply touch that message.

Scroll through your email just like you scroll through a web page.

Zooming in

Just like browsing the web, you can "Zoom in" to see your email in larger text. You can "Double Tap" (see page 32) just as you did with the web and you can also "Pinch" to zoom in – see page 33.

Reply, Forward or Delete Message

At the bottom of your email-reading pane is a tool bar.

From this you can "**Delete**" it or "**Reply**," "**Reply All**" or "**Forward**" the mail.

NOTE: "**Reply All**" is only an option if there was more than just one recipient to an email.

Replying to an Email

Most likely the "**Reply**" command is the one you will use most often. Just touch the "**Reply**" button.

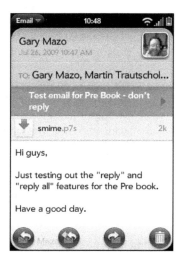

You will now see that the original "Sender" is now listed as the "Recipient" in the "To:" line of the email.

The subject will automatically state: "Re: *(Original subject line)*."

Type your response using the keyboard. When you are done, just touch the blue "**Send**" button at the top right hand corner of the screen.

Using "Reply All"

Using "**Reply All**" is just like using the "**Reply**" function, except all of the original recipients of the email and the original sender are placed in the address lines. The original sender will be in the "To:" line and the other recipients of the original email will be listed on the "Cc:" line.

Using the "Forward" Button

Sometimes, you get an email that you want to send on to someone else. The "**Forward**" command will let you do that.

IMPORTANT - FORWARD ATTACHMENTS:

If you want to send someone any attachments from an email you receive, you must choose "**Forward**." ("Reply" and "Reply All" will not include the original email attachments in your outgoing message.)

When you do touch the "Forward" button. You may be prompted to either "**Include**" or "**Don't Include**" attachments (if there were any) from the original message.

Then, address the message using the same techniques as we showed you above. Type a few letters to select a person from your address book, type an

email address or touch the

icon to find someone from your contact list.

Type a short note if desired, or just press the "**Send**" button to send on the forwarded message.

Deleting Email Messages

As you get more and more comfortable with your Pre as an Email device, you will find yourself using the "Mail" program more and more. It will become necessary to occasionally do some "Email Housecleaning" and delete Email messages you no longer need on your device.

Deleting from the Inbox

Deleting a message from the "**inbox**" is as easy as "touching" the "message bar" and then "sliding" it to the right.

You must also delete it from "TRASH" This action does not delete from the device – it goes into your "**Trash.**" You must then go into your "Trash" folder and "slide" each message to the right to permanently Delete it form the Pre.

NOTE: While the message will be deleted on your device, a copy will still remain on the server.

Deleting from the Message Screen

Another way to delete messages can be found in the "Message Viewing" screen. Just open any message to read. Notice the icons at the bottom of the Screen.

At the bottom right, you will see an

icon of a trashcan. Just touch that icon and the email you are reading will be put into the trashcan and deleted.

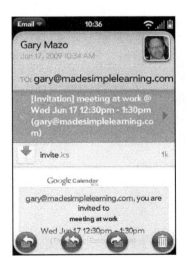

Moving Email Messages

Email Messages can be moved out of your inbox for storage or for reading at another time.

Moving from the Inbox

Just as you did with "Deleting" a message, navigate to your and "Open" the message you wish to move.

Touch the "**Email**" tab in the upper left hand corner or swipe down in that same corner to bring up the drop down menu.

Select "**Move to Folder**" from the menu.

You may not have many folders in which to move your messages, but you will always have a "Trash" option in addition to the "Inbox." If you have a "Gmail" or other IMAP email account, you should see folders similar to those pictured.

Select the "**Trash**" option or any other folder that may be available to you, and the messages will be moved to that location.

Setting your Email Options

There are a few user-configurable options that you can adjust for your Email accounts.

From anywhere in your Email App, just touch the "Email" tab in the upper left hand corner.

Select the **"Preferences & Accounts"** tab and you will be taken to the account and settings page.

Adjusting the Mail Settings

Touch any one of your Email Account names and you will be taken to the "Account Settings" screen.

You can change your "**Account Name**" and "**Full Name**" as you wish it to appear in an email by just touching the editable field and typing in what you wish to see for that account.

Notifications, Sounds and Vibration

The Pre gives you the option of being "Notified" each time an email is delivered. The "Notifications" show up at the bottom of the screen – no matter what program you might be in. See more on "Notifications" on Page 121.

To "Enable" email "icon" to show you notifications, just make sure the "Slider" is set to "On."

You also have the option of having an Email Notification "Sound" and/or "Vibration" of the device when an email is delivered. Set these sliders to either "**On**" or "**Off**" depending on your preference.

Changing your Email Signature

By default, Emails you send will say "Sent from my Pre" unless you change the "Signature line" of the email.

NOTE: You can have a separate signature for every Email Address on your Pre – you adjust them all individually in the account settings as shown above.

Touch the "**Signature**" tab and type in the new Email Signature you want at the bottom of emails sent from the Pre.

You can also adjust the "**Reply to Address**" that will be shown in each email you sent by adjusting the settings (usually not necessary) in the box below the "**Signature**" box.

Changing your Default Mail Account (Sent From)

If you have multiple Email Accounts set up on your Pre, you should set one of them – usually, the one you use most, as your Default account. When you simply select "**Compose**" from the Email screen, the default account is always chosen.

Touch the "**Default Account**" tab and you will see a list of all your Email accounts. Simply Touch the one you wish to use as your "Default Account." The "Default Account" field is at the bottom of your "**Accounts and Preferences**" screen.

When you touch "**Default Account**" all your accounts are listed – just choose the one you wish you use.

Advanced Email Options

You can adjust how many days worth of messages you wish to "Sync" from your mail server and keep on your Pre. You can also adjust the frequency that email is "Pushed" or "Pulled" onto your device.

Changing the "Sync" Options

Touch the Mail account to adjust and then scroll down to "Sync."

The "Default" setting for the "Show Mail" setting is 3 Days.

Just touch the "Show Email" drop down menu and change that to 1 Day, 7 Days, 2 Weeks, 1 Month or All. If you do nothing – it remains set at 3Days.

USE SSL/Authentication

These features were discussed above, but this is another location to access those features for this particular account.

Automatically Retrieve Email

You can set your Pre to "manually" retrieve email (meaning that you tell it when to get the mail, or you can set it to have "New Data" "Pushed" to the device at set intervals.

Having automatic retrieval is very handy if you just want to turn on your Pre and see that you have messages – otherwise, you need to remember to check.

Setting up "Push" options

Touch the "**Get Email**" Tab under the Sync options shown above.

Depending on the type of Email Account, different options may be available. Typically, IMAP email accounts (like Gmail) give you the option of informing you of Email "As items arrive."

Typically, POP 3 Email accounts like those from Comcast and AOL and other ISP's can be "Pulled" to the device in a specified interval.

With the Pre, when you touch the "Get Email" tab you can choose a time interval between 5 minutes and 24 hours.

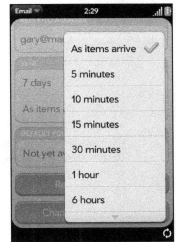

Working with Email Attachments

The Pre allows you to Send and Open popular Email Attachments. Most often on a Smartphone, you will receive an attachment to look at. The Pre makes it very easy to view that attachment and, soon, you will be able to "Edit" the attachments on the Pre.

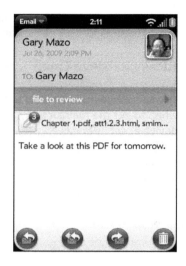

Opening Email Attachments

When you are sent an Email with an attachment, the attachments is indicated under the "Subject" line of the Email. If more than one file is attached, there is a small number indicating the number of attachments.

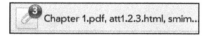

Touch the Attachment you wish you open and it will begin to download. The progress bar will display the download progress.

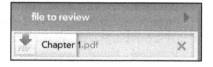

Once the Email Attachment has been downloaded, just touch the "Attachment File" and it will open in the appropriate program.

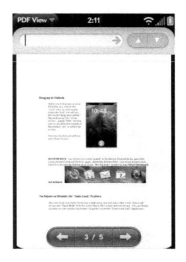

PDF files open with the PDF viewer and Word, Excel and PowerPoint files use the "Document viewer" program.

When you are done viewing the attachment, you can reduce it to a "Card" and just "throw" it off the screen.

Sending Email Attachments

Sending Email attachments is as easy as opening them. Just begin to compose an Email as you did above.

Touch the small "Paper Clip" icon in the lower left hand corner. The next screen has four "soft" keys at the bottom –

the first is for attaching a "Photo," the second is for attaching a "Video," the third is for attaching an "Audio" file and the last is for attaching a "Document."

Touch the appropriate "Soft Key" and simply choose which file you wish to attach to the email.

The file you choose shows up right under the "Subject" line – just like the attached file you just opened above.

Troubleshooting Email Problems

Usually, if you follow all the steps above, your email will perform seamlessly and you will be retrieving, forwarding and composing new emails before you know it. Sometimes, whether it is a server issue or an ISP requirement, email may not be as flawless as we hope.

More often than not, there is a simple setting that needs to be adjusted or a password re-entered.

Checking your Account Settings

Go to "**Preferences and Accounts**" as you did above and then touch the Mail account that seems to be giving you trouble.

At the bottom of the Account Settings page is a tab that reads "**Change Login Settings**." Touch that tab and the Advanced Email Options are displayed.

Check that the "Incoming Mail" settings are the same as those provided to you by your ISP.

If you received an error message while trying to "Send" an email, the issue will be most likely in your SMTP settings – the settings that the email program uses to access your mail server to send mail.

Scroll down to "Outgoing Mail Server" to see the settings used for "Sending" Email. Make sure that these, as well, are exactly as provided by your ISP.

Using SSL

Some SMTP servers require the use of "**Secure Socket Layer**" ("**SSL**") security.

If you are having trouble sending email and the "**Encryption**" switch is set to "**None**" try setting it to "**SSL**" and see if that helps.

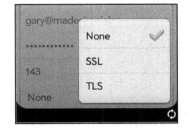

Changing the Server Port

Most often, when you configure your Email account, the server port is set for you. Sometimes, there are "tweaks" that need to be made that are specific to your ISP.
If you have been given specific settings from your ISP, you can change the server port to try to alleviate and errors you might be receiving.

To change the server port, go back to the specific   settings for your account. Touch the tab for the "Port", as you did in the previous step.

Type in the correct number provided by your ISP. When you are done, just perform the "Back" gesture.

Email Is Not Being Sent

Sometimes, you need to adjust the outgoing "Port" for Email to be sent properly. As you did above, go into "**Preferences and Accounts**" and touch the tab for you Email account and then touch "**Port.**" Try a different port setting for the "Outgoing Server Port." Try 587 or 995 or 110. If those don't work, contact your ISP to get a different port number.

Can't Open Email Attachments

The "Mail" app on the Pre can handle many types of attachments that may come through via email – but not all. The attachments supported on the Pre are:
> .doc and .docx (Word Documents)
> .htm and .html (web page)
> . ppt and .pptx (PowerPoint Presentations)
> .txt (text files)
> .xls and .xlsx (Excel Spreadsheets)

Make sure your attachment is not some other, non-supported format type.

Chapter 11:
Messaging (Text and Media)

SMS stands for Short Messaging Service and it is commonly referred to as "Text Messaging." MMS stands for "Multi-Media Messaging" or simply "Media Messaging" (usually when pictures or audio are included as part of each message). Text messages are usually limited to 160 characters and are a great way to quickly touch base with someone without interrupting them with a voice call. And usually demand a more immediate (and shorter) response than an email message. Sometimes you can text someone and receive a text reply when it would be impossible or difficult to place a voice call.

Combined Messaging App

One of the great things about the Messaging App on the Pre is that it allows you to combine many forms of messaging in a single unified inbox:
- Text (SMS Text Messaging),
- Instant Messaging (AOL Instant Messenger, Google Talk, etc.), and,
- Media Messaging.

SMS Text Messaging on your Pre

Text messaging has become one of the most popular services on cell phones today. While it is still used more extensively in Europe and Asia, it is growing in popularity in North America.

The concept is very simple; instead of placing a phone call – send a short message to someone's handset. It is much less disruptive than a phone call and you may have friends, colleagues or co-workers who do not own a Pre or other smartphone – so email may not be an option.

One of the authors uses text messaging with his children all the time – this is how their generation communicates. "R u coming home 4 dinner?"

"Yup." There you have it – meaningful dialogue with a seventeen year old – short, instant and easy.

Setting Up More Instant Messaging (Text Messaging) Accounts

When you start using the Messaging Icon the first time, you will be asked if you would like to setup additional Messaging accounts.

At publishing time, you could setup a Google Talk and AOL Instant Messenger account. We believe it is likely that other services will be available by the time you read this book.

Click "Add an Account" to add more accounts to your Messaging Icon.

Click "Done" to get started and send your instant messages (SMS Text Messages).

Composing SMS Text Messages / Instant Messages

Composing an SMS message is much like sending an email. The beauty of an SMS message is that it arrives on virtually any phone and is quite simple to reply.

Composing an SMS Message from the "Messaging" icon

There are a couple of ways to start your SMS messaging App. The easiest is to just touch the Messaging Icon.

When you first start the SMS App you most likely won't have any messages, so the screen will be blank. Once you get started with SMS messaging you will have a list of messages and current "open" discussions with your contacts.

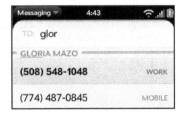 Touch the "Compose" icon in the lower left corner of the screen.

The cursor will immediately go to the "To" line. You can either start typing in the name of your contact or just touch the "+" button and search or scroll through your contacts.

When you find the contact you wish to use, just touch the name and now their name will appear in the "To:" line.

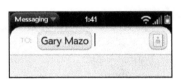

Type in your message with the keyboard at the bottom and then

touch the "**Send**" button.

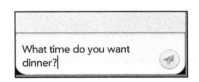

Options after sending a text message

Once the text has been sent, the window changes to a "threaded" discussion window between you and the contact. Your text that you sent is in a Green text bubble. When your contact replies, their message will appear in a Blue bubble.

To leave the SMS screen, just "**Swipe Up**" and reduce the application to a "**Card**." You can then keep the card "**Open**" or "**Swipe**" up and "**Throw**" the card away to close the program altogether.

You can send another text just as you did before or you can also view their **"Contact info."** Touch the name in the top "Bar" of the "Messaging" screen and the "Contact Info" will be displayed.

From the "Contact Information" you can place a phone call, send an email – even "Poke" them on facebook.™

Composing an SMS Message from "Contacts"

You also have the ability to start the SMS App and compose an SMS message from any contact in your Pre.

Just find the contact you wish to "text" by searching or scrolling through **"Contacts."**

Next to each phone number is an **"SMS"** icon. Just touch that SMS box and the **"Messaging"** app will load.

NOTE: Remember that you can only send SMS messages to a mobile number.

Choose the number and follow the steps above.

Replying to a Text Message

When a Text message is received, your Pre will play an indicator tone or vibrate or both – depending on your settings. A notification icon will show up in the lower portion of the screen.

When you see and/or hear the indicator, just touch the "Notification" icon

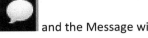 and the Message window will open up.

Viewing Stored Messages

Once you begin a few threaded messages, they will be stored in the "Conversations" section of your "**Messaging**" application.

Start the "**Messaging**" App and touch "**Conversations**" at the top to see your current discussions.

To continue a conversation with someone, just touch on that "thread" and it will open up showing you all the past messages back and forth. Just touch the text box, type in your message and touch the "**Send**" button to continue the conversation.

SMS Notification Options

There are a couple of options available to you with regards to how your Pre reacts when an SMS message comes in.

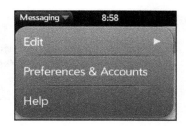

Start your "**Messaging**" App and touch the "**Messaging**" tab in the top left-hand corner. A new sub-menu will appear in a grey box with the options: "**Edit**," "**Preferences and Accounts**" and "**Help**." Touch "**Preferences and Accounts**."

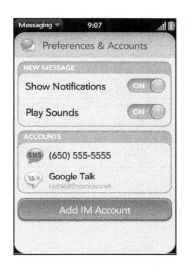

There are two "switches" – one to "**Show Notifications**" and the other to "**Play Sounds.**"

Move the slider to either the "**On**" or "**Off**" position to make changes in the settings.

NOTE: When "**Show Notifications**" is "**On**" the Messaging notice will display as a pop-up at the bottom of the screen.

Multi Media Messaging ("MMS")

Pre users also have the tools to send and receive Multi-Media Messages – picture messages. MMS messages appear right in the messaging window like your SMS text messages.

SOME CARRIERS DO NOT SUPPORT MMS: Make sure your carrier supports MMS and that it is included in your plan or else you could be in for a surprise when you bill comes.

Starting an MMS Message Thread

Touch the "Messages" icon to start messaging – just like you did with SMS.

Choose your recipient as you did on page 198

Type your message at the bottom, just like you did before.

To attach a picture to the message, touch the "Paper Clip" icon

 in the lower right hand corner.

Once you touch the "Paper Clip," you will see the list of available photos on the phone which can be used as a Multi Media Message.

Touch one of the picture folders and choose a photo to use.

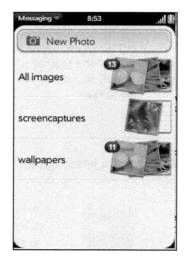

To take a photo, choose "New Photo" and follow the instructions on page 225.

Touch the photo to use and it will immediately move to the threaded messaging window with a small "x" showing (in case you want to change the picture.) Just touch the "x" and follow the steps above to choose a different photo.

Touch the "**Send**" button. You will then notice that the picture is now displayed much larger in the midst of the threaded message with that particular contact.

The message thread can have both a combination of SMS and MMS messages displayed – which is a great feature.

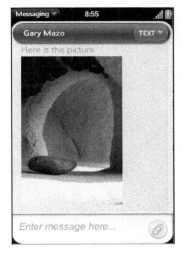

Choosing a Picture from "Photos" to Send via MMS

The second way to send an MMS message is to just go straight to your "**Photos**" App and choose a picture.

Start your "Photos" App and navigate your pictures as you did on Page 234. To only send ONE picture, just touch the picture you wish to send and then touch the

"send" icon  in the upper left hand corner. You will now see MMS as the second option.

There are five options listed for you - Choose Share via MMS and the photo will load into the "Bubble" just as above.

Type in your message, as you did above, and then touch the "**Send**" arrow in the lower right-hand corner. The photo will now be a part of the message thread to that particular contact.

Deleting a Message Thread

There may be times when you wish to delete a complete message thread. Fortunately, this is very easy to do on the Pre.

Open your "Messaging" application and scroll to the thread you wish to "Delete." Touch and "Throw/Swipe" the message thread to the right and you will see a red "Delete" button. Touch the "Delete" button and that particular message thread will no longer be listed in your threaded conversations.

Chapter 12:
Surfing the Web

Web Browsing on the Pre

You can browse the web to your heart's content via Wi-Fi or with your Pre's 3G or Wi-Fi (when available) connection. The Pre has quite a nice feel for a mobile web browser. Web pages on the Pre load fairly quickly and look like Web Pages on your computer. With the Pre's ability to "Zoom" in, you don't have to worry about the small screen size inhibiting your web browsing experience.

Launching the Web Browser

By default, the "**Web**" icon is located at the top of your first Launcher Page. If you use the Web a lot, you might want to consider moving the icon to your "Quick Launch Bar" – see page 242.

Touch the Web icon and you will be taken to the "Home Page" of your browser. Most likely, this will be the Pre Home page – but you can change that – we will show you how in just a few pages.

The initial Pre Home page is essentially your "Bookmarked" web pages with actual images from those pages showing as icons.

206

Layout of the Screen

Touch one of the icons (Bookmarks) to see a typical Web Page.

How can I see the web address?

As you look at your screen, you should notice that the "Address Bar" is at the top of the screen.

This displays the current name of the web site – tap the address bar and it will display the actual web address.

At the bottom of the screen are 2 or 3 icons; "**Back**," "**Forward**" and "**Refresh**" or "**Reload**" page rounded arrow.

NOTE: If this is the first web page you are viewing, there will not be a "**Forward**" button – just a "**Back**" one.

Typing or Searching for a Web Address

The first thing you'll want to learn how to do is to get to your favorite web pages. You can do this in a couple of ways.

Typing a Web Address

You can type the web address (URL) just like on your computer's web browser address bar. To start typing, tap the address bar at the top of the browser. Type the web address using your keyboard and press the Enter key or tap the "Arrow" key next to the web address to go to that page.

You can also type in that web address from the "Home" page of bookmarks at the top of the screen.

Searching for a Web site Name

Because the Pre uses a "Universal Search," you can type in a few key words of the web site name and then you will have the option to choose a "Google" Search or "Wikipedia" search for the name.

If you have visited the site before or a related site, those entries will appear below as part of your Web History.

Tap any of the rows that pop up below where you are typing to select that entry.

In the example above, we tried a "Google" search for the first two words of our web site "Made Simple."

This was not enough to find our site, so we tried "Made Simple Learning" and we turned up as the first entry.

Booking Your Travel Reservations

There are several travel web sites that you can use to book your airline, hotel and rental car on your Pre.   Orbitz (www.orbitz.com) and Travelocity (www.travelocity.com) are just a couple of examples.

You can double-tap or use the pinch open/pinch closed to view the web page larger or smaller. (See pages 32 and page 33.)

The other option is to use an "App" specifically designed for travel reservations. To locate the App, start up the **App Catalog** icon and perform a search to find Apps that specialize in "travel reservations." Learn more in our chapter on the "App Catalog" starting on page 320

Typing a New Web Address While Viewing A Web Page

Normally, if you start typing on your keyboard while viewing a web page, you will see your characters appear in the top address bar as shown. This makes getting to a new web page very easy. Type the web address and hit the Enter key, or type a few search terms and tap the search item that pops up.

The only exception is when your cursor happens to sitting inside a field in a web form on the page you are viewing. If you start typing, then you will be filling in that field. As we show here, in the "From" field on this travel site page.

All you need to do in this case, is tap outside the web form to move the cursor off the web form. Or, you may swipe down a couple of times to get to the top of the web page. When you swipe down enough, you will see the web address bar appear at the top. Then you can start typing.

Moving to Backwards or Forwards through Open Web Pages

Now that you know how to enter web addresses, you will probably be jumping to various web sites. The "**Back**" and "**Forward**" arrows at the bottom of the page make it very easy to advance to pages just visited in either direction. You can also always use the "Back Gesture" as well.

Let's say you were on the New York Times Web site looking at the news and then you want to jump over to ESPN.com to check sports scores. As long as your cursor is not in a web form field, simply type 'espn.com' and press the Enter key to get to ESPN.com.

To go "Back" to the NY Times page, hit the "**Back**" arrow. To Go "Forwards" to the ESPN site again, tap the "**Forward**" arrow.

Adding Bookmarks, Add Icon to Home Screen, Mail Page Links

Just like on your computer, you can set "**Bookmarks**" on your Pre. To add a new Bookmark, simply touch the "**Web**" tab at the top left of the web screen to bring up the menu.

Choose **"Add Bookmark"** to add a new bookmark.

You could also add this Web Page to your "Launcher" screen or "Share" it with a friend.

Tap the "Page" menu item and choose **"Add to Launcher Screen"** (puts a handy icon on your home screen), or **"Share"** which will allow you to email the link to the current page to anyone.

After you touch **"Add Bookmark"** you may edit the name of the bookmark (the web address is shown underneath the editing window.)

We recommend shortening longer web names and making them unique so they are easier to recognize in your Bookmarks List.

Press "**Add Bookmark**" to save your changes.

Accessing Your Bookmarks

Once Bookmarks are set, to view your Bookmarks, simply bring up the menu by touching "Web" in the upper left corner (or swiping down in the same corner) and select "**Bookmarks.**"

Editing and Deleting Bookmarks

When you first touch the "**Bookmarks**" menu item, you will see a "Bar" or row for each "Bookmark."

To go to a Bookmarked site: Tap that Bookmark bar anywhere except on the

Just scroll through the Bookmarks to go to any page in your list.

You can change the Name of your Bookmark at any time. Just touch the small "*i*" on the right side of each bookmark entry.

Now you may edit the Bookmark name or URL (web address).

Just type a new name or URL and choose "**Save Bookmark**" at the bottom.

Deleting Bookmarks

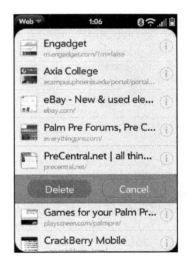

To Delete the bookmark, simply "Slide" the Bookmark to the right and you will see the "**Delete**" button pop up. Touch "**Delete**," confirm the Delete and the bookmark will no longer be in your menu.

To Re-Order Your Bookmarks

Just touch and drag a Bookmark "Up" or "Down" the list to change its place. Release the Bookmark and it will now reside in a new location.

Clear or Erase All Your Bookmarks

You may decide that you want to "start over" and "Clear" all you bookmarks.

From the "Bookmarks" page, bring up the menu by tapping the "Web" tab in to top left corner. Then touch "**Clear Bookmarks**."

All your Bookmarks will disappear.

Using the New Card Button

On our home computers, many of us have come to rely on "tabbed" browsing which allows us to have more than one web page open at a time so we can quickly move from one to the other. The Pre uses the system of "Cards" as discussed on Page 26.

Just touch the "Web" tab from any Website to see the menu. Touch "**New Card**" and then either choose one of your bookmarked pages or type in a new web Address as you did above.

TIP: Put your Web Icon in the Quick Launch Bar (see page 242) and use the "Launch Wave" to Open a new Web Card.

The first time you touch this button, you notice that the web page you are currently viewing disappears. It is really just reduced to a "Card" for later access.

Switching Between Cards

Perform the "Swipe Up" Gesture to reduce the second Webpage to a "Card" and you will now see that the first Webpage is also a "Card" on your Home Screen. You can just move between the "Cards" and touch one of them to bring it to the foreground.

Zooming in and Out in Web Pages

Zooming in and out of web pages is very easy on the Pre. There are two primary ways of zooming; "Double Tapping" and "Pinching."

Double Tapping

If you tap twice (double tap) on a column of a web page, the page will zoom in on that particular column. This makes it convenient to zoom in on exactly the right place on the web page. This is helpful on pages that are not specifically formatted for a mobile screen.

To "Zoom Out" just "Double Tap" once more. See graphically how this looks on page 32.

Pinching Open or Pinching Closed

"Pinching" is a technique you can use in Web Pages and in Pictures to "Zoom" in on a particular section of the page. It takes a little bit of practice, but will soon become second nature.

See graphically how this looks on page 33.

Use your thumb and forefinger and place them close together at the section of the web page you wish to zoom into. Slowly "Pinch out" –

separating your fingers. You will see the web page then zoom in. It takes a couple of seconds for the web page to "focus," but it will zoom in and be very clear after a short while.

To "Zoom Out" to where you were before, just start with your fingers apart and move them slowly together – the page will zoom out to its original size.

Activating Links from Web Pages

Often times, when surfing the Web, you will come across a "link" that will take you to another web site. Because the Web Browser is a fully functioning browser, you can touch the link and you will jump to a new page.

If you want to return to the previous page, press the "Back" arrow as shown earlier.

Web Browser Copy and Paste

In the Web Browser on the Pre, you can copy images from a Web page and save them to your "Photos" directory or send then via Email or MMS.

TIP: The same technique will work to copy images from email messages you receive.

NOTE: Many of the same keyboard shortcuts will work as we showed you in the Copy/Paste section on page 48.

Initiate the Copy

In any web page or in any Email message, hold down the "Orange" key and tap any image on the screen. A pop up will appear asking you to either "Share the Image" or "Copy to Photos."

Sharing the image via email

Select "Share the Image" and your Email App will start with the picture from the Web shown as an attachment along with a message that will automatically generate; something like: "Here's a picture I think you will like."

Adjust the Subject and Body of the Email and send it with the paper airplane button in the lower right corner.

Copy Image to Photos

Instead of **"Sharing the image"** choose **"Copy image to Photos"** and the image from the Web will go into your "Photos" app. The new photo will go into the "Miscellaneous" directory in your "Photos" App.

The Pre will display a message letting you know the image was successfully copied to your "Photos" App.

NOTE: If the photo you are copying is "linked" to another web page, you will see additional options on the screen: **"Open in a New Card," "Share Link"** or **"Copy URL"** are displayed as additional options.

Copying and Pasting Text from a Web Page

You can easily copy and paste text from a web page and then paste it into an email or other user-editable field in pretty much any App in which you can enter text.

Initiating the Copy

On any web page, hold down the "Shift" key and touch the screen. A small "Yellow" dot will initially appear and then the paragraph you are touch will become highlighted.

TIP: The Shift Key is also the key to start selecting text in a document you are editing such as an email, calendar event, or contact.

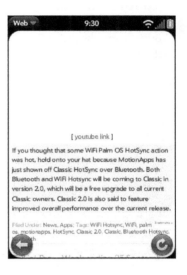

Select All

To Select all the text on the page, bring up the menu by tapping the "Web" tab in the upper left corner, then touch "Select All."

TIP: The shortcut to do this is touch and hold in the Gesture Area and press the letter "A" on your keyboard. You will see all the text on the web page become highlighted in Yellow.

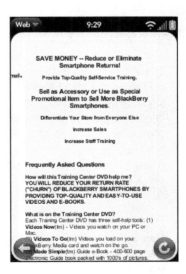

Copying Text

Copying text is handled the same way as we showed you on Page 48.

Either touch the "Web" tab in the upper left hand corner, touch the "Edit" tab and choose "Copy" or hold the "Orange" Button and the letter "C" to copy the text.

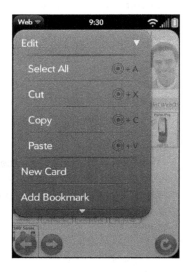

NOTE: you can copy additional text by keeping your finger on the "Shift" key and touching additional paragraphs on the page.

Pasting Text

Go into any application where text can be entered – Email, Memos, Calendar and place the cursor in the location where you wish to paste text.

Touch the MENU in the top left corner (in the Email App it is just says "Email") and touch the "Edit" tab and choose "Paste." Alternatively, you can hold the "Orange" button and the "V" key (think CTRL V or CMD V on your PC or Mac.)

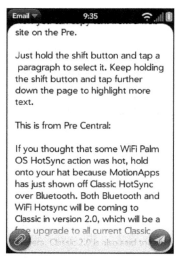

How can you copy something buried inside a paragraph of text?
TIP: If you want to copy something, say a Street Address or email address that happens to be buried in a paragraph of text in an email message or web site, then you will need to first select and copy that entire paragraph.

Next, go to the Memos icon and paste it into a new memo. Now, since you can edit the text, use the Copy/Paste instructions on page 48 to copy just what you want or need out of that paragraph of text.

Adjusting Web Browsing Preferences

Like other "Settings" we have adjusted so far, the settings for the Web Browser are found in the menu in the top left hand corner.

Touch the "Web" menu, scroll down to "**Preferences**" and touch.

Block Pop-ups, Accept Cookies, JavaScript

Three "Sliders" are present – one for each:
"**Block Popups**," "**Accept Cookies**" and "**JavaScript**."

The "Default" setting is for each of these to be in the "**On**" or "**Yes**" position.

Some Websites may give you an error message telling you to either "Enable" or "Disable" one of these options – move the slider to the "**OFF/ON**" or "**YES/NO**" as needed.

Speed Up Your Browser: Clear History & Clear Cookies

On the bottom of the Web settings screen, you will see the "**Clear History,**" "**Clear Cookies**" and "**Clear Cache**" buttons.

If you notice your web browsing getting a bit sluggish, that might be a good time to go and clear out the "**History,**" "**Cookies**" and "**Cache**."

Each button your touch will give you a "Confirmation" screen to perform the selected action.

TIP: It is also a good privacy measure to prevent others from seeing where you have been browsing.

Occasionally, it is a good idea to clear out your history and your cookies.

Using Browsing History To Save Time and Find Sites

The advantage to keeping your frequently visited sites in the history is that you can load them from the "History" tab when you go into the "Web" menu in the upper left hand corner.

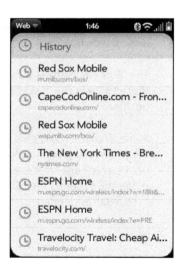

TIP: Sometimes you know that you want to go back to a certain site, but you can't remember the name – checking the history will show you the exact site you wish to visit.

NOTE: You can also "Clear" your history from the "History" screen. Just touch the "**Web**" tab in the upper left hand corner and then choose "**Clear History**."

Chapter 13:
Camera

Your Palm Pre comes with a 3.0 Mega Pixel camera. It is easy to take pictures, file them and send them (via email and Multi-Media Messaging) or even instantly upload and share with your friends on your facebook™ or Photobucket account.

Starting the Camera

The "**Camera**" icon should be on your first page of icons inside the Launcher – usually on the first screen at the top right. If you don't see it, then flip left or right until you find it. (See page 21 for help with the Launcher.)

Geo-Tagging

Geo-Tagging is a feature that puts your geographical GPS (Geographic Positioning System) coordinates into the picture file. If you upload your pictures to programs like **facebook®** or **photobucket®**, the coordinates of your picture can be used for your friends to see exactly where the picture was taken.

In order to use Geotagging, you must turn on make sure a few settings are switched correctly. To do this, tap your "**Location Services**" icon, roll down and make sure both "**Auto Locate**" and "**Geotag Photos**" are set to "**ON.**"

Taking a Picture

Tap the Camera Icon to start it. Once your camera is on, center your subject in the screen of your Palm Pre.

Can I Zoom In?
No. As of publishing time, the Palm Pre did not allow you to zoom in – we anticipate this will be changed in the future.

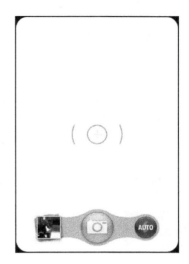

When you are ready to take a picture, touch the "Camera" button along the bottom. You will hear a shutter sound and the screen will indicate that the picture is being taken.

Once the picture is taken, you will see the small "Photo Roll" window in the lower left hand corner change to show the picture "on top."

Rapid Fire Pictures (About 1 per Second)

If you want to take a lot of pictures in a hurry, press and hold the Space Key. This will allow you to take about 1 picture every second. Great for 'rapid fire' shots when you want to catch action scenes.

Press and hold the Space Key to take 'rapid fire' pictures (about 1 every second).

Using the Flash

There are not many user changeable setting on the Pre camera. You can change your flash from the default

 = AUTOMATIC

"**Automatic**" setting to either
"**Always On**" or "**Off**."

To the right of the "Camera"
button in the picture-taking
window, you will see the small
symbol for the flash. Just touch
the symbol to change "**Auto**" to
the sign for "**Flash On**" or
"**Flash Off.**"

 = ALWAYS ON

 = ALWAYS OFF

Taking a Picture of the Phone's Screen (Screen Captures)

Say you just got your highest score on your favorite game and you wanted
to share it with your friend… or you saw something curious on your screen
and wanted to save it… or you simply wanted to take a picture of the
screen to help teach people how to use their phone.

You can take a picture of your Pre screen by pressing 3 keys
simultaneously:
Orange Key + Sym Key + "P."

Where are these stored?

Your 'screen shots' will be stored
inside a '**Screen Captures**' folder
in your "Photos" icon.

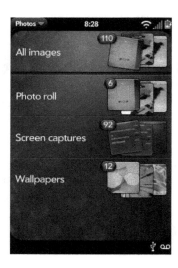

Viewing Pictures you have Taken

Your Palm Pre will store pictures you take on the Palm Pre in what is called your "**Photo roll**." You can access the Photo Roll from inside both the Camera and Pictures icons. In the Camera, touch the "**pictures**" icon in the bottom left corner of the camera screen.

Once you touch a picture to view, you can "**Swipe**" through you pictures by touching the screen and swiping left or right.

To get back to the photo Roll, use the "**Back**" Gesture.

To take another picture, reduce the "Photo" App to a "Card" by swiping up or pressing the "Center Button." Your Camera should already be an "Open Card," swipe left or right to bring it to the center and then touch the Card to go back into the Camera.

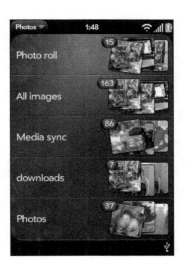

Viewing from "Photos" Icon

You can also view the pictures taken by your camera in your "**Photos**" Icon.

Tap the Photo Icon (see page 234 for help) and you will see a new Photo Album called "**Photo roll**." Once you tap Photo roll, you will see all the pictures you have taken.

Tap any picture to view it. Remember the "Pinch Open" and "Pinch Closed" finger motions to zoom in and zoom out of your pictures (see page 238)

Deleting a Picture from the Photo Roll

Deleting a picture from the "**Photo Roll**" is just like deleting a picture for any Photo album. Touch any picture from your Photo Roll and then touch

the small "**Trash Can**" icon  at the top right of the screen.

Confirm the "**Delete**" and the photo will be deleted from the phone.

Emailing a Photo, Assigning to a Contact, Use as Wallpaper

With every picture you have, you can do many things with it. Tap this

"arrow" icon  in the upper right hand corner when you are viewing the picture to Assign to Contact, Set it as Wallpaper, Share via Email, Share via MMS or Upload to facebook® or Photobucket® or other Picture Sharing account.

Assign to a Contact

Find a Photo from your "**Photo Roll**" that you wish to use as a "Contact" photo for someone in your address book.

Open the Photo, and touch the icon in the top left corner and choose "Assign to Contact."

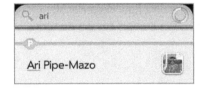

Navigate through your contacts and find the right contact for the photo. You can either swipe through your contacts or start typing the first name + (space) + last name on the keyboard.

Once you find the Contact, open it up by touching it.

Drag the picture to move the square around the part of the picture you wish to use as the contact photo.

TIP: Zoom in or out as needed using the 'finger pinch' method (See page 238).

When you are done, touch the "**Set to Contact**" button.

You should see the notification at the bottom letting you know the picture is being set to the contact.

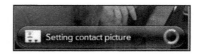

To double check, open your contacts and find the contact whose picture you just set. It should reflect the new photo.

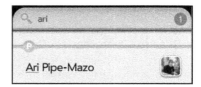

Set as Wallpaper

Touch the icon in the top left hand corner and then touch "**Set as Wallpaper**." You now see your picture with a large "Set Wallpaper" button at the top. Just touch the "**Set Wallpaper**" button and your picture now becomes the "Wallpaper" for your phone.

You should see a small notification at the bottom of the screen letting you know that the wallpaper has been set.

Share via Email

Once again, just locate the picture you wish to share via email. Touch the picture, and touch the icon in the top left corner and choose "**Share Via Email**." Your "Photo" App will be reduced to a "Card" and your Email will be launched.

Choose the recipient by either typing in their name and then locating the correct contact and email address or touch the "**Contacts**" icon in the top right and scroll through or type to find the appropriate contact.

NOTE: if the email address is not in your contacts, you may simply type in a full email address and it will be put in the "To" line of the email.

Type in the "Subject" and then the "Body" of the message and touch the small "Send" icon in the lower right hand corner.

Share Picture via MMS

MMS stands for "Multi Media Message." Essentially, this is sharing a photo as a "Picture Message." It is different from sending as an Email attachment in two ways: (1) The picture is imbedded right in the message (instead of as an attachment, and (2) Some of your friends and colleagues may phones that cannot receive email but those phones may be able to receive MMS – so it is more versatile than email.

Open the picture you wish to send (as you did above) and touch "**Share via MMS**." Learn more about MMS on page 201.

The "Messaging App" will open. Just type in the name or touch the contact icon and scroll through your contacts to find the individual to whom you wish to send the picture.

Enter your message in the lower line and then touch the "send" icon – that's all there is to it. You will then see your picture in a threaded message chain with this contact.

NOTE: MMS MAY COST EXTRA -- Some wireless carriers (phone companies) will charge you extra to send MMS and SMS (Text Messages). Check with your carrier for any additional charges before you send too many MMS pictures.

Upload a Picture

Open the picture, touch the icon and choose "Upload."

If you have already setup a facebook or Photobucket account and logged into it from your Palm Pre, then you will be able to simply tap "Upload" and then select the account. If you have not logged into your account from your Pre, then it will prompt you to login the first time by selecting "**Add an Account**."

If you don't have an account, you will need to set one up on either the facebook™ (www.facebook.com) or photobucket™ (www.photobucket.com) web sites from your computer.

After you have setup an account, enter your login information and upload your picture.

Chapter 14:
Photos

Photos on your Pre

Due in large part to the beautiful screen on the Pre, viewing pictures is a joy. Using the touch screen interface makes navigating, zooming and manipulating your photos lots of fun.

The images look so amazing on the Pre because it actually has a higher pixel density (more dots per inch) than your regular laptop or computer monitor.

Launching the Photos Icon

If you like using your "**Photos**" Icon, you might want to place it in your Quick Launch Bar for easy access (see page 242). To get started with photos, touch the "Photos" Icon.

The first screen shows you the various Photo Albums or Libraries. These were created when you set up you Pre and Synced with your computer (iTunes or another software).

On Page 85, we showed you how to choose which photos to Sync with your Pre. As you make changes to the library on your computer, they will be automatically updated on your Pre.

Choose a Library

From the Photo Albums page, touch one of the Album tabs to show the photos in that Album.

We touched the "Photo Roll" collection and immediately the screen changed to show us thumbnails of the pictures in this library.

Tap and drag your finger up and down to view all the pictures. You can flick up or down to quickly move throughout the album.

Working with Individual Pictures

Once we locate the picture we want to view, we just tap on it to view it. The picture then loads into the screen.

NOTE: Usually, your pictures will not take up the full screen on your Pre especially if they were shot in "Landscape Mode."

TIP: The picture to the right was shot in "Landscape Mode," so to see it in full screen you will have to tilt your Pre on its side.

Moving Between Pictures

The "Swipe" gesture shown on
page 27 is used to move from one
picture to the next. Just "Swipe"
your finger left or right across the
screen, and you can move through
your pictures.

TIP: Drag your finger slowly to
slowly move through the picture
library.

When you read the end of that
particular library, just perform a
"Back" Gesture and you will return
to the thumbnail page of that
particular album.

To get back to your main Photo
Album page, just perform the
"Back" Gesture one more time.

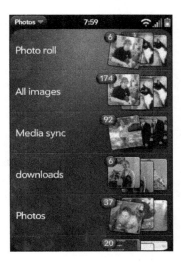

Zooming in and Out of Pictures

As described in the "Getting Started" section of the book, there
are two ways to Zoom in and out of pictures on your Pre: "Double
Tapping" (page 32) and "Pinching" (page 33).

Double Tapping

As the name describes, this is a quick "Double tap" on the screen to "Zoom
in" on the picture. You will be zoomed in on the spot where you double
tap.

In the example above, we wanted to get a better look at the "bench" in this photo. So, we double tapped on the bench and the photo zoomed to that location.

See page 32 for more help on Double-Tapping. To "Zoom out" just "Double Tap" once more.

Pinching

Also described in the "Getting Started" chapter on page 33, "Pinching" is a much more precise form of zoom. While "Double Tapping" only zooms in or out to one set level, "Pinching" really allows you to "Zoom" in or out just a little bit or quite a bit.

To "Pinch," hold your thumb and forefinger close together and then slowly (while touching the screen) separate them – making the picture larger. To "Zoom in" just start with your thumb and forefinger apart and move them together.

NOTE: Once you have activated the "Zoom" by either method, you will not be able to "Swipe" through your pictures until you return the picture back to its standard size.

To end the slide show, just tap the screen. You can adjust the duration of each picture as well as the Transition, Repeat and Shuffle settings.

Using a Picture as Your Pre Wallpaper

Your Wallpaper is the picture that comes on as soon as you "Wake" or turn on your Pre. On page 248 we showed you how to change your Wallpaper. You can always set your wallpaper to be one of your pictures from your collection.

Emailing a Picture

As long as you have an active network connection, either with the cellular networks (see page 20 to understand network connection symbols), or a Wi-Fi Connection (page 130) you can send any picture in your photo collection via email.

Assign Picture to a Contact

On page 139, we talked about adding a picture when editing a contact. You can also find a picture that you like and choose to assign it to a contact from the "Photos" Icon. First, find the photo you want to use.

As we did with Wallpaper, and Emailing the Photo, tap the Options button – the one furthest to the left of the top row of soft keys. If you don't see the icons, tap the screen once.

With the picture open, tap the screen to bring up the icons at the bottom of the screen. Activate the Photo "Options" – the icon on the top left.

Touch the "**Assign to Contact**" button.

Choose "Assign to Contact"

You will see your "Contacts" on the screen. Just start typing the name of the contact you desire with your keyboard (See page 140 for Contact searching tips.)

Once you find the contact to which you would like to add the picture, touch the name.

You will then see the "Set to Contact" screen. Tap and drag the picture to move it and use the pinch to zoom in or out.

When you have it just as you want, touch the "**Set To Contact**" button to assign the picture to that contact.

NOTE: The nice thing about the Pre is that the Photos App will still be open – just reduced to a Card. Once the photo is set to your contact, "Swipe" up to reduce the Contact App to a "Card" as well.

Deleting a Picture

You will notice that the "Trash Can" icon is visible at the top of any photo. Simply touch the "Trash Can" and you will be prompted to confirm the "Delete" of the photo.   Accept the "Delete," then the photo will delete from your Pre.

If you don't see the top row of icons, tap the photo once to activate them. Then tap the "Trash Can" icon. You will be prompted with the option to "Delete" the picture.

Touch "**Delete**" and the picture will be deleted from your Pre.

Send Picture as MMS - Multi-Media Message

Tap the "**Send**" icon to bring up the menu and select "**Share via MMS**" and the picture will be placed inside a threaded message. Look at page 203 where we show you exactly how to do this.

Chapter 15:
Moving Icons

Your Pre is very customizable; you can move icons around, have your favorite four icons located in the Quick Launch Bar and adjust the look and feel so it suits your tastes.

Moving Icons to the Quick Launch Bar - "Locking Them"

When you turn your Pre on, you will notice that there are five icons "locked" on the Quick Launch Bar. The "Standard" four icons locked to the Quick Launch Bar are: "**Phone**," "**Contacts**," "**Mail**," "**Calendar**" and "**Launcher**."

Now, you might decide that you wish to change one or more of these to an App that you use more often. Fortunately, moving icons to the Quick Launch Bar is easy.

Starting the Move

The first thing you need to do to move a new icon into your "Quick Launch Bar" is to make space for the new icon in the bar. That means that you have to move one of the icons out of the Quick Launch Bar before you can move another one into the bar.

Touch and hold your finger over the icon in the Quick Launch Bar you wish to replace. You will notice a sort of "halo" around the icon indicating it can now be moved.

Drag the icon into the launcher page of icons – wherever you would like it to reside. You should now only have four icons in the Quick Launch Bar.

What we want to do is replace the "**Calendar**" icon with our "**Web**" icon, so the first thing we do is hold and move the "Calendar" icon up a row – out of the Quick Launch Bar.

Next, we locate the "**Web**" icon and move it down to the Quick Launch Bar – notice that it is sort of transparent until we "set" it into place.

When we are sure that we have the icons just where we want them, we simply release the icon and "lock" it into place. Now, we have the "**Web**" icon in the Quick Launch Bar where we want it.

Moving Icons to a Different Icon Page

Your Pre puts up to 27 icons on a "page" and these pages can be found by just "Swiping" (right to left) on your home screen. With all the cool Apps available, it is not uncommon to have several pages full with icons.

Sometimes, there is an icon you rarely use that may be on your first page and you want to move it way off to the end page. This is very easy to do and is handled in a very similar fashion to the "moving" icons to the Quick Launch Bar discussed above.

Touch and Hold any icon to initiate the "Moving"

Touch and hold the icon you wish to move. In the images that follow, we want to move my "**Tasks**" icon to the last page – it is one App we don't use as much as the others.

Touch and hold until you see the 'halo'. Then drag the Icon off the page to the left or right.

Then, Drag and Drop the Icon On To another Page

Touch and hold the "**Tasks**" icon and drag it to the right. We will see all the pages of icons move by and when we get to the last page, we just "release" the icon and it is now placed at the very end.

After dragging to a new page, release the Icon when you are ready to 'place' it.

Deleting Icons

It is as easy to delete an icon as it is to move it. One thing to remember, however, is that when an Icon is deleted, we are actually deleting the program from our Pre. This means you won't be able to use the Icon again without re-installing or re-downloading it.

Press and Hold Orange Key to Initiate "Deleting"

We have learned that the "Orange" key serves many functions on the Pre. It is the Orange key that will help us "Delete" an icon (actually the program) from the Launcher.

NOTE: You can only delete icons (programs) that you have downloaded to your Pre – the pre-installed icons and programs cannot be deleted.

While you are holding the "Orange Key" Just tap the icon you would like to delete. You will be prompted to select either "**Delete**" or "**Done**." If you select "**Delete**," the icon is then removed from your Pre.

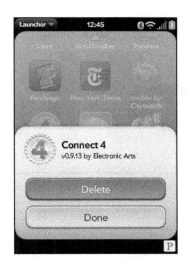

Delete from Launcher Screen

Touch the "**Launcher**" icon in the "Quick Launch Bar" or press the "Center Button."

Touch the "**Launcher**" tab in top left hand corner. Touch "**List Apps**" and all of your applications will be listed.

Just "Slide" the application bar to the right and choose **"Delete"** or **"Done"** as you did above.

Resetting All Your Icon Locations (Factory Defaults)

Occasionally, you might want to get back to the original or 'Factory Default' icon settings.   An example of when you might want to do this is when you have moved too many new Icons to your first page and want to see all the 'basic' Pre icons again.

To do this, locate and tap on your "Device Info" icon. It is usually in the third screen of the Launcher.

Scroll to the bottom of the screen. You should see the **"Reset Options"** button at the bottom.

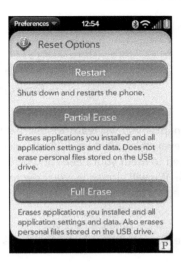

Now touch the "**Partial Erase**" button. Touch this and any additional programs and icons on your Pre that were installed will now be removed.

NOTE: This does not remove personal information or "Wipe" the device – we cover that on Page 328.

Chapter 16:
Personalize

In this chapter you will learn some great ways to personalize your Pre. You can change everything from your "Wallpaper" to sounds and more. Many things can be fine-tuned to meet your needs and tastes -- to give your Pre a more "personal" look and feel. We will also show you how to secure your Pre with either a 4-digit passcode or a password.

You can also personalize how your Pre rings – see page 118 for selecting a new Ringtone, or page 119 to learn how to use any song (MP3) for your Ringtone.

Also, if you want to get more advanced, you can personalize how the phone rings for a specific person in your Contact list – say your special friend, spouse or even, ugh, your boss.

You may see that some of your contacts already have pictures attached – for example Facebook contacts who have pictures in Facebook, will also have pictures on your Pre. You can easily add a picture to any contact who you want to – see page 139.

Changing your Wallpaper

When you first turn on your Pre or "wake" it up, you will see your "wallpaper" behind the "**Drag Up to Unlock**" button. You will also see your wallpaper behind the phone when you are in a call. When you first turn on your Pre, you might not have any wallpaper set or it might be just black with the clock.

There are a couple of ways to change your wallpaper on the Pre. The first way is very straightforward.

Changing Wallpaper from the "Screen and Lock" icon

Touch the **"Screen and Lock"** icon then touch the **"Change Wallpaper"**

tab and you will see a screen showing you the Wallpaper folder, the Photo Roll (if you have taken pictures with your Pre) and folders for your photo library and any other libraries you might have synced in iTunes or with another Media program.

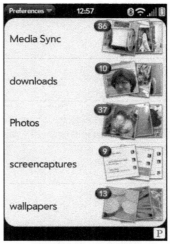

Touch any of the Albums displayed, or tap the **"Wallpaper"** tab to see all the pre-loaded wallpapers for the Pre. Tap the picture that you desire and a preview screen will appear.

If you wish to select the picture shown as your wallpaper, touch **"Set Wallpaper."**

If you don't want to use that picture, just use the "Back" gesture and choose another photo.

Change Wallpaper from any Picture

You can also touch your "Photos" icon and you will see your picture albums.

Touch the Photo album you with to look through. When you find a photo that will work for you, just "Touch" it and it will open in your screen.

Touch the photo and in the top left hand corner of the photo is the "**Set as**" icon. Just touch that icon and five options pop up on the screen, the second one being "**Set Wallpaper**."

Touch the "**Set Wallpaper**" button (as you did above,) the picture will be properly scaled for your screen.

Security Options

Your Pre can hold a great deal of your valuable information. This is especially true if you save information like Social Security Numbers and Birth Dates of your family members. It is a good idea to make sure that someone who picks up your Pre can't access all your information. Also, if your kids are like ours, they might just pick up your cool Pre and start surfing the web. You might want to enable some security restrictions to keep them safe.

Setting a Passcode -- a Password or PIN to Lock Your Pre

Touch the "**Screen and Lock**" icon and then the "**General**" tab. Now scroll down to tap on the "**Secure Unlock**" item.

You have three options – "**Off**," "**Simple PIN**" or "**Password**."

When you choose "**Simple PIN**" you will see a familiar 4-digit pin with number pad. Just type in a 4-digit Pin and then confirm your choice by typing it again.

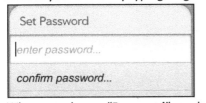

When you choose "**Password**" you have the option of typing a more secure "**Password**" for your device.

Now, when you look at the "**Secure Unlock**" item, it will reflect either the "**Simple PIN**" or "**Password**" option you selected for security.

To make changes in these settings (like turning the passcode off) you will be prompted again to enter your code.

Advanced Gestures

Slide the "Switch Applications" button to the "On" position to enable Advanced Gestures. Enabling "Advanced Gestures" will enable swiping the entire length of the Gesture Area to switch to the next or previous App.

Chapter 17:
Playing Music

Your Pre as a Music Player

Your Pre is such a capable device that you might forget that it is also a very capable music player. Your Pre plays, organizes, randomizes and allows you to view, listen and customize pretty much every aspect of your music.

Music and Video on the Pre

Music on the Pre is handled through the "**Music**" icon on the home screen.

Touch the "**Music**" icon and the contents of your music library are displayed for you.

Simply choose whether you wish to view your music collection by "**Artisits**," "**Albums**," "**Songs**," "**Genres**," "**Playlists**" or "**Amazon MP3**" (to view music files purchased through the Amazon music store. See page 270.

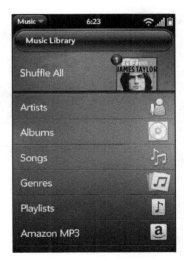

Searching For Music

In every view in "Music" (Playlists, Artists, Genres, Songs, etc.) you can search for a particular "Song" or "Artist" by just sliding out the keyboard and beginning to type – that's all there is to it.

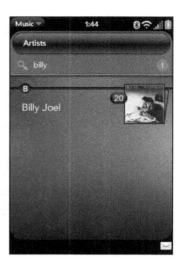

In this example, we wanted to search "Artists" for Billy Joel, we type "Billy" and the artist's name shows up with the number of songs my Pre has by that particular artist. (Showing 20 songs.)

Artists View

To see the "**Artists**" view of your music, just touch the "Artists" tab

and you will see "**Artists**" at the top of the list.

To see your music displayed by "**Album**" or **Song**" or "**Genre**" – just touch the corresponding tab.

Touch the Album, Song or Genre you wish to play and your music will begin playing.

Albums View

Your Pre can also organize your music by Albums when you Touch the "**Albums**" tab.

Again, you can "Search" through the list by just typing the name of an Album or just by scrolling through the list. Once you choose an album, all the songs on that album will be listed.

Songs View

Touching the "**Songs**" tab will show you a listing of every song on your Pre.

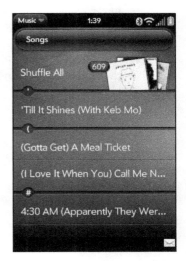

If you know the exact name of the song you desire, just type the name of the song into your keyboard and "Matching Names" will then be displayed.

Playlists View

Playlists are created in iTunes or another Media Manager program on your computer and then Synced to your Pre.

How can I create a Playlist?

Learn how to create playlists on page 86

A playlist is something you create and can be made up of a particular genre, artist, year of recording or any collection of songs that interest you.

Once a playlist is synced to your Pre, it shows up in the "**Playlist**" view. In this example, we touched the "Classic Rock" playlist and all the songs from that playlist are listed.

To go to a different Playlist, we use the "Back" gesture and choose another Playlist.

Genres View

"**Genres**" view will group similar music together by style – like "Rock" or Country" or any one of a number of different musical styles.

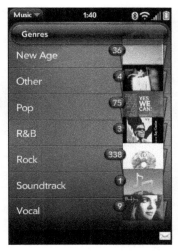

You can choose a Genre and play through all the songs or just one particular song in that Genre by touching the corresponding song.

Shuffle All

In every view, the top most option is to "**Shuffle All.**" Just like it sounds, if you touch this tab, all the music in the grouping you have selected will begin to play in a random order.

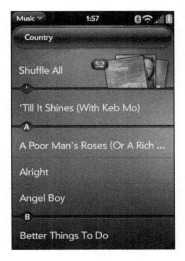

In this example, we selected "Country" as our Genre and then "**Shuffle All**." You can see the "Grouping" – in this case the "Genre" shown in the title bar.

Once the song starts playing, you will notice that the "Shuffle" icon is filled in, indicating that we are in Shuffle mode.

Playing your Music

Now that you know how to "find" your music, it is time to "Play" it. Just touch the song name and it will begin to play.

The screen shows a picture of the Album from which the song originates and the name of the album at the top.

Next to the Album name is the "**Cover View**" and "**List View**" icons.

Along the bottom is the name of the song, the "**Play/Pause**" Key and the "**Next**" and "**Previous**" Buttons.

To either side is the "**Shuffle**" icon on the left and the "**Repeat**" icon to the right.

Pausing and Playing

TIP: Touch anywhere on the screen to Pause or Play your song.
You may also touch the "**Pause**" symbol (if your song is playing) or the "**Play**" arrow (if the music is paused) to play or resume your song.

= PAUSE

= PLAY

To play the "Previous" or "Next" song

If you are in a "Playlist," touching the "**Next**" arrow (to the right of the Play/Pause button) will advance you to the "Next" song in the list. If you are searching through your music by "Album," touching next will advance to the next song on the album.
Touching the "**Previous**" button will do just the reverse.

NOTE: You can also just swipe left or right to move to another song.

To Rewind or Fast Forward inside a Song

In order to fast forward within the current song, press and hold the "Next" arrow.

= **Press & Hold to Fast Forward**

To Rewind, press and hold the "Previous" button.

= **Press & Hold to Rewind**

Adjusting the Volume

To adjust the volume on your Pre: using the external volume buttons on the left-hand side of the Pre.

Press the "**Volume Up**" key (top of the two) or the "**Volume Down**" key to raise or lower the volume key. You will see the Volume indicator appear and show you the relative volume.

Volume Keys

Cover View vs. List View

The "Default" view for Music is to show you the Album Art or Cover View of the song playing.

If you touch the "**List View**" icon, the view changes to show you just the name of the song and the artist and the elapsed time of the song. A Blue Bar fills as the song plays and nears the end.

TIP: In list view, to play a different song, simply touch it.

Repeating and Shuffling

In the "Play" mode, you can activate additional controls by simply "tapping" the icon in the lower status bar. Tap "**Repeat**," to hear the song or Playlist or other grouping repeat. Tap "**Repeat**" again and a small number "1" appears letting you know just the song will be repeated. Tap "**Shuffle**" and if you are in a "**Playlist**," "**Album**," "**Artist**" "**Song**" or "**Genre**" view, all the songs in that group will be shuffled.

Repeat One Song and Repeat All Songs in Playlist or Album

To repeat the song you are listening to over just touch the "**Repeat**" symbol at the bottom left of the top controls twice until you see it turn blue with a "1" on it.

To repeat all songs in the playlist / song list or Album, touch the repeat icon until it turns blue (and does not have a "1") on it.

To turn off the Repeat feature, just press the icon until it is no longer highlighted.

Shuffle Icon

If you are in listening to a "Playlist" or "Album" or any other category or list of music, you might decide that you don't want to listen to the songs in their prescribed order. Touching the "**Shuffle**" symbol will then "re-arrange" the music in a random order of play.

Reduce Music Player to a "Card"

Using the "Swipe Up" Gesture, you will reduce the Music Player to a "Card" which can stay open while you multi task and use any other program.

To enter the Music Player again, just touch the Card on your Home Screen.

Search for Other Songs by Artist

Because the Pre is "Constantly Connected" it is has access to the Internet at all times. Touch the "**Music**" tab in the top left-hand corner and you can see several options available to you.

Search Amazon MP3

To look to purchase more music by this artist, just touch the "**Amazon MP3**" tab.

Then touch the "**Search for**…." Tab and you will be taken to the Amazon MP3 Store with a listing of other songs by that artist.

The Amazon MP3 store will open in another "Card." You can scroll through the songs and choose to purchase music right on your Pre. Look at Page 271 for details.

To reduce the Amazon Music store to a "Card" just "Swipe up." To go back to the Music Player, just touch on its Card.

Search YouTube

To look for videos by or about this artist, just touch "**YouTube**" and then touch one of the search options shown to you.

Just like above, a new "Card" will launch – this time with the YouTube Player and a listing of available videos to watch.

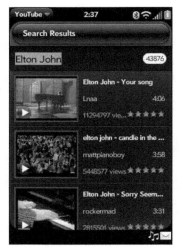

You can choose a video to watch, and it too, will load in another "Card." When you are done, just use the "Back" gesture to go back to the listing or use the "Swipe Up" Gesture to minimize the YouTube App to a Card.

REMEMBER: Once you are in Card View, just "Throw" the card up to close the program.

Chapter 18:
Amazon MP3 Store

Getting Started with Amazon MP3 on the Pre

Earlier in this book we showed you how to get your music from your computer into your Pre (see page 73). One of the great things about the Pre is that it is easy to buy music and listen to your purchases in minutes right on your Pre.

The Pre allows you to access the Amazon MP3 Store (the mobile version) right on the device. All you need is your cellular phone network connection or a Wi-Fi network connection in order to access the Amazon store. After you purchase or request free items, they will be downloaded to your Pre and can easily be transferred back to your computer via USB or Media Sync mode – see Page 81.

Starting Amazon MP3

When you first received your Pre, Amazon MP3 was one of the icons on the second Home screen page. Touch the Amazon MP3 Icon and you will be taken to the mobile Amazon Store.

NOTE: Amazon "App" does Change Frequently

Since Amazon MP3 is really a web site, it is likely to change somewhat between the time we wrote this book and when you are looking at it on your Pre.

Setting up your Amazon MP3 Account

The first time you try to use
the Amazon MP3 store, you
will see a screen asking you to
accept the Amazon MP3 terms
and service.

Next, sign into your Amazon
account with your email
address and password. If you
wish to be able to purchase
songs without having to enter
your password, just "turn on"
the "**Enable 1 Click®**" feature.

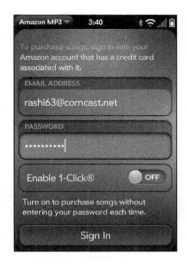

Navigating the Amazon MP3 Store

Amazon uses similar icons to
other programs on the Pre, so
getting around is quite easy.
There is a drop down menu at
the top and categories at the
bottom. You can also use the
Pre's "Universal Search" to just
start typing what you might be
looking for.

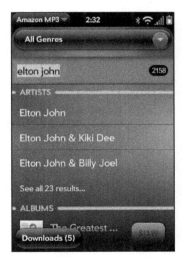

Scrolling is just like scrolling in any other program; just tap the screen and drag your finger up or down to look at the selections available.

New Releases, Albums, Artists and Songs

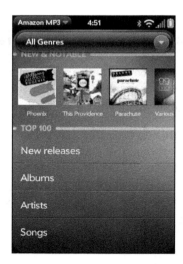

Under the Search Bar and the "**New and Notable**" section of the music store are a series of "Top 100" categories to make it easy to find the music you are searching for. There are four main categories to search through; "**New Releases**," "**Albums**," "**Artists**" and "**Songs**."

New Releases - "The Newest Stuff"

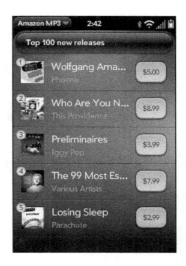

If you like to see what is brand new in a particular category, you will want to browse the "New Releases" category. Tap "New Releases" and the top 100 New releases will be displayed.

One note - these are often a combination of "full albums" and "digital 45's" or other short compilations.

Albums –

Touch "Albums," and the top 100 albums in whatever Genre you have selected will be displayed. If you don't specify a particular "Genre" from the drop down menu, the top 100 albums in all Genres will be shown.

Artists and Songs –

Just as you did above, touch either "Artists" or "Songs" in either "All Genres" or in a particular Genre to display the top 100 selections.

GENRES - "TYPES OF MUSIC"

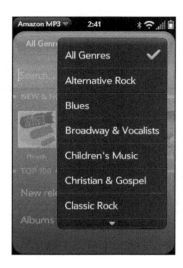

Touch the "**All Genres**" drop down to browse music based on genre. This is particularly helpful if you have a favorite type of music and would like to browse just that category.

There are dozens of "Genres" to browse – just scroll through the Genres and then touch a particular genre to start your search.

Go ahead and browse through the music until you see something that you would like to preview or buy.

Searching for Music

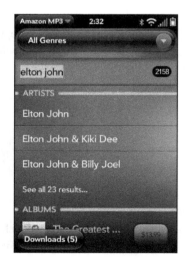

One of the very cool things about the Amazon MP3 Store is that you can just start typing on your keyboard in any category, "**Albums**," "**Songs**," "**Artists**" or "**New Releases**." You can also search in any of the Genres from the Drop Down menu.

In this example, we are in the "**All Genres**" category searching for "Elton John."

We know that we are looking for a particular song of his, but we cannot remember the name. So, we switch to the "**All Songs**" tab and search for "Elton John." Now we find the song we were looking for – "Levon" – which we will show you how to purchase in the next section.

Purchasing Music

Once you locate a song, video, TV show, or album, you can touch the "**BUY**" button. Then your media will start downloading.

We suggest you view or listen to the "**preview**" unless you are absolutely sure you want to purchase the item.

Previewing Music

Touch either the title of the song or the "Album Art" to the left of the Song title and you will hear the first 30 seconds of the song. The "Tab" will start to "fill up" as the preview progresses.

Touch anywhere in the tab and the preview will stop.

Purchasing a Song or Album

Once you are sure you want to purchase a song, video or other item, touch the price of the song or the "**BUY**" button.

The button will change and turn into a green "**BUY**" button.

Tap the "**BUY**" button.

Touch the Amazon MP3 Tab at the top left and choose "**Downloads.**" You can monitor the progress of your latest download as the "Tab" fills up showing the progress of the download.

When the download is complete, you will see a "Check Mark" next to the name of the song.

Chapter 19:
Viewing Videos

Your Pre as a Video Player

The Pre is not only a capable Music player; it is a great portable Video Player. The Widescreen, fast processor and Operating System make watching anything from Music Videos to TV Shows and full-length motion pictures a real joy.

Loading Videos on Your Pre

You can load Videos on your Pre just like your music, through iTunes from your computer (see Page 79) or look at one of the other third party solutions for video transfer on page 81.

Watching Videos on the Pre

Click on your "**Videos**" icon to see the videos on your Pre. Just touch the movie you wish to watch.

Playing a Video

Touch the Video you wish to watch and it will begin to play.

Most Videos take advantage of the relatively large "screen real estate" of the Pre and they play in widescreen or landscape mode. Just turn your Pre to watch.

When the Video first starts, there are no menus, no controls and nothing on the screen except for the video.

To Pause or Access Controls

Touch anywhere on the screen and the control bars and options will become visible. Most are very similar to those in the Music player. Tap the "**Pause**" button and the video will pause, tap that same button to play.

Fast Forward or Rewind the Video

The Pre Video player does not offer specific Fast Forward or Rewind controls. Instead, the Video Player uses a simple "Time Bar" to let move around in the video.

The Pre does take advantage of "Gestures" to help you get around a video. Use a short "**Swipe**" of the screen to move you "**Forwards**" or "**Backwards**." So, a short "**Swipe**" from left to right – or "**forwards**" will advance the video by 30 seconds.

TIP: A short "**Swipe**" from right to left – or "**Backwards**" will rewind the video by 30 seconds.

Using the Time Bar

At the bottom of the Video screen is a "Slider" which shows you the elapsed time of the video. If you know exactly (or approximately) at which point in the Video you wish to watch, just hold and drag the slide to that location. Some people find this to be a little more exact than holding down the Fast Forward or Rewind Buttons.

Changing the Size of the Video (Widescreen vs. Full Screen)

Most of your Videos will play in widescreen format. However, if you have a video that was not "converted" for your Pre or is not "optimized" for the screen resolution, you can touch the "expand" button, which is to the right of the upper Status bar.

You will notice that there are two arrows. If you are in "Full Screen" mode, the arrow is pointing up to the larger box. If you are in "Widescreen" mode, the arrow is pointing down toward the smaller box.

In a Widescreen movie that is not taking up the "Full Screen" of the Pre, touching this button will "Zoom in" a bit. Touching it again will "Zoom out."

NOTE: if you are watching a properly formatted, widescreen movie, touching this button will not do anything to alter the size of the screen. Only if you are watching a "Letterbox" or standard 4 x 3 format will the video change to fill up the screen. Be aware, that just like on your widescreen TV, when you try to "force" a non-widescreen video into widescreen mode, sometimes, you will lose part of the picture.

Deleting Videos

Deleting via USB Drive

To Delete a Video from your computer (to save space on your Pre) you must connect you Pre to your PC or Mac and choose "USB Drive"

When you see the "USB" drive on your Mac desktop or the "PALM PRE" disk drive in Windows Explorer, double click to look at the files on your Pre.

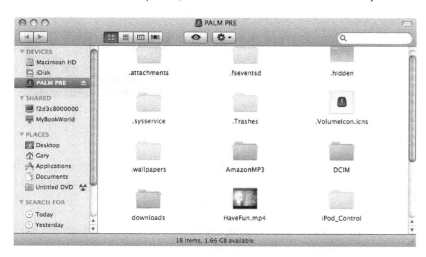

You should see your Video files in the window. Click to highlight the video file and either drag to your "Trash" (Mac) or "Recycle Bin" (Windows) or choose the "**Edit**" menu and select "**Delete**."

HaveFun.mp4

Deleting via Media Sync Mode

If you added the video using "**Media Sync**" mode (see page 73) then you will need to "Delete" the video file via "**Media Sync**" mode as well.

Media Sync

Select "**Media Sync**" when you connect the Pre to your PC or Mac and then your Media program will launch.

Name	▲	Time
☑ TheDarkKnight_PC_EN 1		2:32:12

Go to wherever your Movies are stores in your Media Player (this screen shows iTunes version 8.2 or lower) and locate the Movie.

Highlight the Movie or Video, go to the "Edit" menu and select "**Delete**" or press the "**Delete**" key on your keyboard.

Undo	⌘Z
Cut	⌘X
Copy	⌘C
Paste	⌘V
Delete	
Select All	⌘A
Select None	⇧⌘A
Special Characters...	

Watching TV Shows on your Pre

Some wireless carriers (like Sprint in the US) stream TV shows to the Palm Pre. Sprint calls their service "Sprint TV," but if you are on another wireless carrier, check for something similar.

TIP: You may find that the free "Kids" or "Family" TV shows are a fantastic way to keep your young ones busy during a long car trip!

Chapter 20:
Fun on Your Pre

Your Pre excels at many things. It is a multi-media workhorse and it can keep track of your busy life as well. One area where the Pre really excels is as a "Media" workhorse.

This is evident when you fire up the Pre version of YouTube or stream Internet Radio via the Pandora App in the App Catalog.

YouTube on your Pre

Watching YouTube videos is certainly one of the most popular things for people to do on their computers these days. Fortunately, this is one activity that you can take "on the road" with you. YouTube is as close to you as your Pre.

Right on your Launcher, usually on the first screen, is a YouTube icon. Just touch the YouTube icon and you will be taken to the YouTube App.

Searching for YouTube Videos

When you first start YouTube, you usually see the "**Popular**" videos on YouTube that day.

Just scroll through the video choices as you do in other Apps.

Using the Bottom "Videos" Button

At the bottom of the YouTube App is the "**Videos**"

button. Touch this button and a short menu pops up allowing you to see the "**Popular**," "**Most Viewed**" or your Video "**History**."

To see the videos that YouTube is "Featuring" that day, just touch the "**Popular**" icon. To see those videos that are "**Most Viewed**" online- just touch the "**Most Viewed**" icon.

You can search the huge library of YouTube videos by touching the "**Search**" icon. Just touch the search box as in previous Apps, and use the keyboard to type in your search term. Type in a phrase, topic or even the name of a video.

In this example, we are looking for the YouTube Video of the President's inauguration speech – so we type in "Obama Inauguration" and we see the list of videos to watch from the search results.

"More" Options

Touch the title of the Video for which you wish more information – be careful not to touch the video itself or it will start playing.

touch the "**More**" icon and you see a pop up menu for "**More from This Author**" and "**Related Videos.**"

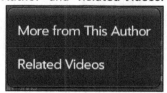

Touch either option to see more "Related" content to view through YouTube.

Playing Videos

Once you have made your choice, just touch the video you want to watch. Your Pre will begin playing the YouTube video in "Landscape" mode.

Video Controls

Once the video begins to play, the on screen controls disappear so you just see the video. To stop, pause or activate any other options while the video is playing, just tap the screen.

The on screen options are very similar to watching any other video. Along the top is the Slider showing your place in the Video. To move to another part in the Video, just drag the slider.

Share Video

When you are done watching the video, just perform the "Back" gesture. The next screen shows the full description of the video you just watched. You also have the option to send the video link (via email) once again by touching the "**Share**" button at the bottom right of the screen.

Touch "**Share**" and then choose whether you wish to send the video via Email or SMS text Message.

Checking and Clearing your History

Touch the "**Videos**" icon in the lower left hand corner and then touch the "**History**" tab. Your recently viewed videos appear. If you want to "**Clear**" your history, just touch the "**Clear**"

button. To watch a video from your history, just touch it and it will start to play.

Pandora® Internet Radio

Growing out of the music Genome project, Pandora® Internet radio is a great way to listen to the music that you want anytime you want it. You could simply load up all your favorite music into the Pre and use the built in Music player as we showed you on Page 255. Pandora® is different, though.

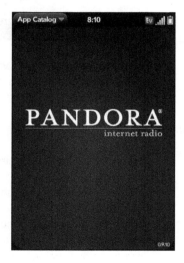

Imagine carrying around every song you like in your pocket – that's Pandora®.

Set Up your Pandora Account

The first step to enjoying Pandora® is to setup your account. You can do this on your Computer (Mac or PC) or right on the Pre. On your Computer, go to www.pandora.com and create an account. You will be asked to generate a user name and password – just choose something you will remember.

Download the Pandora® App

As you did on Page 317, go to the App Catalog and search for the Pandora®
App. Locate the App and touch "**Download**" to install the App onto the
Pre.

Build your Stations

The beauty of Pandora® is that
you build stations based
around the music that you like.
You can choose from some
"Pre arranged" stations or you
can simply enter in an artist's
name (On the Pre or the
Computer) and Pandora will
"build" a station around that
artist.

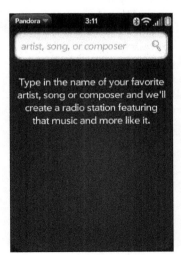

Using Pandora®

Launch the Pandora App from the Pre. Pandora will immediately load the last station you played. If this is your first time using Pandora, Pandora will ask you to either sign in or create a new account.

To Pause the current song, just touch the "Play" key along the bottom row.

To "Skip" the song and go to the next song, just touch the "Skip" arrow at the far bottom right hand location.

To give a particular artist or song a "Thumbs up" or "Thumbs Down" just touch the corresponding icon. If you give a song or artist a "Thumbs Down" Pandora will remember to never play that song or artist on that particular station again.

Bookmark or Purchase Song

Touch the "Arrow" key between the "Thumbs" and a pop up menu shows on the screen.

You can "Bookmark" the song or artist for easy reference in the future by touching the appropriate tab.

To "Buy" the song or album, just touch one of the "Buy" buttons and the Amazon MP3 Store will launch and take you right to that song or album.

See all your "Stations"

Touch the "Stations" button

in the top left and the view will switch to show you all your "Stations." To change a station, just touch one of the tabs and the new station will begin playing.

To add a new station, tap the "+" sign and type in the name of a new artist.

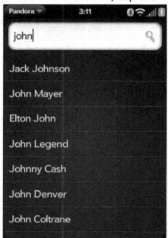

Get Artist or Song Info

Touch the small "I" at the right of the title bar to get information on the particular artist or song you are listening to. Just perform a "Back" gesture to back to the main screen.

Changing Preferences

Touch the "Pandora" tab in the top left hand corner and choose "Preferences" from the drop down menu.

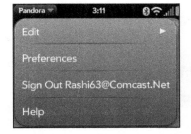

You can then decide to opt for a "higher quality" stream. Choose this is you are in a Wi-Fi hotspot or have strong 3G service. You can then enjoy even better sounding streaming internet radio!

Chapter 21:
Google Maps

Getting Started with Google Maps

The beauty of the Pre is that the programs are just meant to work with one another. We have already seen how your Contacts are linked to the "**Google Maps**" Icon.

Google Maps is the leader in mobile mapping technology. With "Google Maps" you can locate your position, get directions, search for things nearby, see traffic and much more.

Simply touch the "**Google Maps**" icon to get started.

Determining your Location

When you start the "Map" program, you can immediately have maps show you and move to your current location. Tap the small circle next to the Menu.

Maps might ask to use your current location – just touch "**OK**" or "**Don't Allow**."

We suggest choosing "**OK**" to make it much easier to find directions from, or to, your current location.

Changing the Map View: Satellite View

The "Default" view for "Maps" is a basic map view with generic background and streets shown with their names. Maps can also show you a Satellite view.

To see the "Viewing" Options

Touch the "**Menu**" button in the lower right hand corner. Several options are presented to you. If you touch "**Satellite**," the view will change to a Satellite view of the terrain.

Checking Traffic

Your "Google Maps" icon does have the ability to check traffic in many, but not all, areas.

Just touch the "**Menu**" button in the lower right hand corner and then select the "**Show Traffic**" button from the options shown.

On a highway, if there is a traffic situation, you will usually see "Yellow" instead of green – sometimes, the yellow might be "flashing" to alert you to a traffic situation.

Traffic will be shown using colors to indicate the speed that traffic is moving:

> Green = 50 MPH or more
> Yellow = 25 – 50 MPH
> Red = Less than 25 MPH
> Gray = no traffic data is
> currently available

Search for Any Location, Local Businesses, Theaters, Plumbers, More

If your location cannot be determined by tapping the "My Location" button, or you want to map a specific address, city or other point of interest, touch the "Search" bar at the top of the program.

Type in your address, point of interest, or town and state you would like to map on your Pre.

GOOGLE MAPS SEARCH TIPS:

Enter just about anything in the search:
- First Name, Last Name or Company Name (to match your Contacts)
- 123 Main Street, City (Some or all of a street address)
- Orlando Airport (find an airport)
- Plumber, Painter, Roofer (any part of a business name or trade)
- Golf courses + city (find local golf courses)
- Movies + city or zip/postal code (find local movie theaters)
- Pizza 32174 (Search for local pizza restaurants in zip code 32174)
- 950 W. Maude Ave., Sunnyvale, CA 94085 (Palm, Inc. Headquarters)
- 95014 (Zip Code - Apple Computer Headquarters in California, USA)
- N2L 3W8 (Postal Code for RIM - BlackBerry Headquarters in Canada)

Mapping Options Once the Address is Mapped

Now that your address is on the "Map" screen, there are a number of options available to you.

Touch the "**Results**" List to see the full list of entries that turned up after the search.

You can get directions to that location or get Directions from that location by touching the Menu button and then choosing "**Get Directions**."

Or, you can touch on the entry you wish to learn about and choose "**Directions to Here**" from the options listed.

You can also "Add" the address to your Contacts or Call the phone number (if listed in the search results.

In the example below, we touched the phone number from Google Maps and our Phone App launches. Then, we touch "**Add to Contacts**" from the bottom of the phone screen so the Contacts App will launch. We add the name, other information and save the Contact.

Zooming In and Out

You can zoom in and out in the familiar way of "Double Tapping" and "Pinching." To Zoom in by Double Tapping, just double tap on the screen as you would in a Web page or Picture. (See pages 32 and 33)

Getting Directions

Perhaps one of the most useful functions of the "Maps" program is that you can easily find directions to or from any location. Let's say we want to use our current location and get directions to our friend Martin's house.

TAP THE MY LOCATION BUTTON FIRST

If you want to find directions to or from your current location, and you don't have to waste time typing your current address, make sure to locate yourself by tapping

the "My Location" button in the lower right next to the Menu button. You may need to repeat it a few times until you see your blue dot on the screen.

Type in a "Destination" in the search field of Google Maps.

Designate "Start" and "End" location

In this example, we typed in "Fenway Park" and then touched the "Menu" button and chose "**Get Directions to Here.**"

Directions to here

 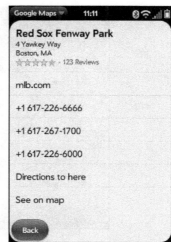

Touch either the "**Directions to Here**" button as you did above or touch the "**Menu**" key and select "**Get Directions**."

Directions will then be shown on the "Map View" or if you touch "Directions List" you can see a list of the directions.

Looking at the Route

Touch the "Arrow" button in the upper right hand corner of the screen and the directions routing begins. Because this is a long trip, there are lots of pages to these directions.

Touch the "**Directions List**" button and a text list of directions is displayed for you to follow to your route.

Scroll up and down to view the complete set of directions.

Using the GPS

While Google Maps does not give you spoken turn-by-turn directions, if you have allowed the GPS to locate you, then the GPS will "Follow" you along the trip. In Map view, the "pages" of directions will turn and the "Blue dot" will continue to track your position along the route.

Chapter 22:
Memos

The Pre handles Memos with a visual bulletin board approach.

Working with Memos is something that will quickly become invaluable on your Pre. Most of us have "Sticky" notes just about everywhere; on our desks, by the nightstand, on the computer...you get the idea.

"Memos" on the Pre give you one, convenient place to keep your notes and simple "to do" lists. You can also keep simple lists like a grocery list or list for other stores like hardware and the pet store. Since you always have your Pre with you, you can add items to these lists as soon as they occur to you and can be accessed and edited at any time.

Getting Started with Memos

Like all other applications, simply tap the "Memos" Icon to start it.

After starting the "**Memos**" App you see what looks like a Bulletin board with "Sticky Notes" upon it.

You might have several Memos – or, if this is your first time with the App, you won't have any at all.

How are my Memos sorted?

You will soon notice that all notes will be listed in reverse chronological order, with the most recently edited notes at the top and oldest at the bottom.

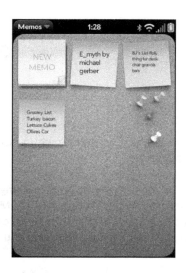

As you add a new Memo, the others will shift place on the screen. So you will notice your notes moving around in order on the screen.

This sorting can be a good thing because your most recent (or frequently edited) notes will be right at the top.

Adding a New Memo

To start a new "Memo," touch the "**New Memo**" note in the upper left hand corner.

Just start typing your Memo.

What is the title of the Memo?
The first 20 or so characters become the defacto "title" of the note, so if you want to make a grocery list, type "Grocery List" and then press the "return" key

and type your items.

Finding, Viewing or Editing your Memos

Your "Memos" appear on the board as "Sticky Notes" to touch. Touch the name of the note you wish to view or edit. The contents of the note are then displayed.

FINDING A MEMO:

To find a specific note, the Pre allows you to start typing with your keyboard. Any note with matching characters (anywhere in the Memo) will be displayed. This makes it very easy to find any Memo. In this example we typed the letters "gr" and only our "Groceries" memo is shown. Notice the matching letters "gr" are underlined:

When you are done reading
the Memo, just perform the
"Back" gesture or "Swipe" up
(or press the Center button) to
reduce the Memo to a "Card."

Editing your Memos

You can very easily edit or change the contents of a Memo. For example,
you might keep a "Grocery List" note and quickly edit it when you think of
something else to add to the list (or when your family reminds you to get
something from the store!)

Touch the "Grocery List" memo, then
touch the screen anywhere and the
cursor moves to that spot for editing.

You can then type new lines of text; you
may use the delete key to delete a word
or a line. (See page 48 for more on copy
& paste.)

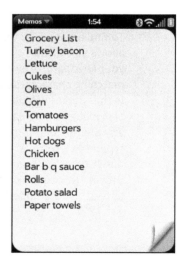

If you hold the "**Shift**" 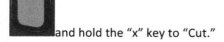 key you
can select and then highlight text - hit
the Delete key to delete a block of text.
Or you can hold the "**Orange Key**"

and hold the "x" key to "Cut."

When done editing, just perform the
"Back" gesture.

Deleting Memos

To delete a "Memo," tap it to open it from the main Notes screen and then touch the "**Memos**" tab at the top left hand corner.

Choose "**Delete**" from the drop down menu and then confirm the "Delete" on the next screen.

Emailing a Memo

One of the very convenient features on "Memos" is the ability to email a memo to someone. Let's say we wrote a grocery note and wanted to email it to our spouse. From the text of the note, touch the "Memos" tab icon at the top of the screen. Choose "**Email Memo**" from the drop down list.

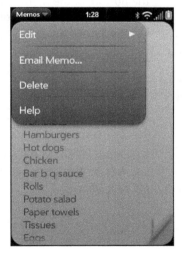

Now we see the "**Compose New Mail**" screen with the subject as "Just a Quick Note" and the body of the message as the contents of the note. Address and send the note as you would any other email.

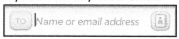

Touch the "To" line of the email, or touch the "**Contact**" icon and find the contact we wish to use.

Changing the Color of your Memo

The Pre gives you the option of changing the color of your Memo. At the bottom of the Memo, the lower right hand corner of the note looks like it is turned up.

Touch this corner of the note and you will see the four available colors for your Memo.

Choose a different color, and the Memo changes to that color. To save your selection, just perform a "Back" gesture and the memo will now reflect the new color on the memo board.

Chapter 23:
Other Apps

The Pre is very useful for a great number of things. Some of the most 'simple' things and apps are those you might find yourself using quite frequently.

You may want to see what time it is in London, Tokyo or any other city around the world. You might want a wake-up alarm clock. How about a daily alarm to remind you of something you do every day? All these can be done in the Clock Icon.

How about calculating the tip on your meal, or other simple, everyday calculations - what would 120 license of our Made Simple videos cost a company at $15.95 each? Use the calculator.

How about the weather for the next few days in your city, or any city in the world. Use the Weather Icon.

For a simple way of keeping track of the your busy life and the various "Tasks" that you need to do, the Pre comes with a handy "Tasks" App.

The Clock

Touch the "**Clock**" icon to launch the Clock.

Immediately, you see the time (based on your Network time) in either Digital or Analog format.

Changing between Analog and Digital

There are not too many options to worry about with the Clock App. One option is to choose the "Theme" of the display. At the time of the writing of this book, there were two themes available; Digital and Analog.

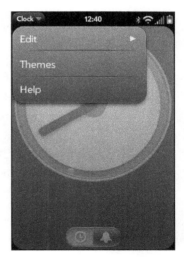

To change the "Theme," touch the "**Clock**" tab in the upper left hand corner and then choose "**Themes**" from the drop down list.

Touch on either "**Digital**" or "**Analog**" and the Theme of the clock will change accordingly.

The Alarm Clock

The alarm clock feature is very flexible and easy on the Pre. You can easily set multiple alarms. For example, you might set an alarm to wake you up on weekdays, and a separate one on weekends. You can even set a separate alarm to wake you up from your Saturday and Sunday afternoon nap at 3:00pm.

To get started, tap the "**Alarm**" button in the lower row of soft keys.

If you have alarms set, they will be displayed. If there are no "Alarms" tap the "**+**" sign in the lower left hand corner to add a new one.

Give your "Alarm" a Name in the "Name" field – choose an easy name that will say, for example "Daily Alarm."

Adjust the time of the alarm by touching either the "**hours**" or "**minutes**" buttons next to the "**Time**" tab. Then, choose either "**AM**" or "**PM**."

If this is a one-time alarm, then set the "Occurs" tab to "**Ring Once.**" A "**Ring Once**" repeating alarm will cause the alarm to automatically be set at "**OFF**" after it rings.

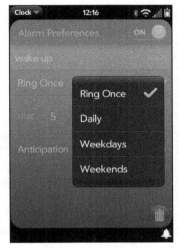

If the alarm does repeat, then adjust the "Repeating" function of the Alarm by touching the "**Occurs**" tab. Touch "**Daily**," "**Weekdays**" or "**Weekends**."

TIP: Use "**Daily**" for your work-week alarm

Adjust the sound the alarm makes by touching the "**Sound**" tab and then choosing an alarm sound from the list.

You may use any of the pre-installed sounds or even "Ringtones" you created on Page 119.

Swipe "Back" when you are done.

To "Snooze" and Alarm, just touch the "**Snooze**" button on the bottom of the screen.
The alarm will ring again in 10 minutes.

You can re-name your Alarm by touching the "**Name**" tab. Use the keyboard and type in a new name for that particular alarm.

Give your alarm a name that is easy to recognize.

Will an Alarm turn on my Pre?

No. If your Pre is completely powered-off (see page 37), the alarm will not turn it back on. However, if your Pre is just in **Sleep Mode** (see page 38), then your alarms will ring just fine.

Calculator App

One more very handy App included on your Pre is the "Calculator" App. The Pre Calculator can handle almost anything a typical family can throw its way; performing both basic and scientific calculations.

Viewing the Basic Calculator

Click on the Calculator icon to start the Calculator App.

In Portrait mode (Vertical) view, the Calculator application is a "basic" calculator. All functions are activated by simply touching the corresponding key to perform the desired action.

Need to store something in memory?

M+ to add it into memory,
MC to clear memory and,
MR to recall the number in memory to the screen.

Viewing More Operations - Percentage and Square Root

Just touch the "Space" bar on your Pre keyboard and the traditional "+" and "-" keys will change to "Square Root " and "%" symbols.

Tap the Space Key to see more operations on the calculator.

The Weather App

 The Pre comes with a very useful and easy to use "Weather" App that is free to download from the App Catalog. Look on Page 320 to see how to download the app.

After you set it up, a quick touch of the "**Weather**" icon will show you the weather forecasts for your area.

It is easy to setup your location and other locations to check their weather on the Weather Icon.

Getting Started with "Weather"

Tap Just touch the "**Weather**" icon. You will most likely be prompted to "Use your Current Location." You can "Accept" that or choose a new location by zip code or name.

Adding a New Location

Just touch the "**AccuWeather**" tab in the upper left corner and choose "Add Location."

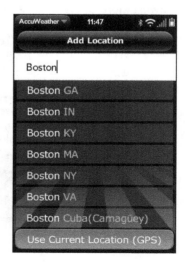

Type in the name of the city or town and then press the "Enter" button on the keyboard.

When you see the town you want, you just touch it.

You will be taken to the main weather screen for the new location.

To Delete a Weather Location

To delete a weather location, touch the "**AccuWeather**" tab in the upper left hand corner and choose "Delete Current Location" from the drop down menu.

Moving Between Weather Locations

Once you have "Weather" set up for your various locations, just touch the main Weather Bar (which has the name of the Current location.)

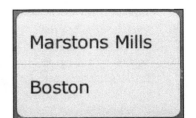

All the available locations will be displayed – just touch on the city you wish to switch to.

Switching to "Celsius"

The "Default" setting is to display the weather in "Fahrenheit." Touch the "**AccuWeather**" drop down menu and select "**Switch to Celsius**" to display the temperature in Celsius.

Different Views in "Weather" App

The normal screen in the "Weather" App shows you the day's forecast in the large area of the screen and the next five days at the bottom. Continue to "Swipe to the left to see the next two weeks of forecasted temperatures.

Changing to Detailed "Hour-by-Hour" Day View

Touch the second icon from the left (which looks like a clock) for a detailed view of today's weather. The main section of the screen how shows a projected temperature and graphic for each hour of the day.
Just swipe to the left to continue to progress through today's full forecast.

Seeing the "Radar" view

Touch the next icon (that looks like a radar) to see the current "Radar View" of the area. The time of the image is noted at the top of the screen.

Seeing the "Indices"

The Last soft key is the "Indices" key, which gives you the weather indices for the day – everything from "Arthritis" levels to "Running" conditions, are displayed in this view. Scroll down the screen to see all the available indices for the day.

You can change the "Indices" view from and "Icon" view to a "List" view by touching the "List" soft key at the top. The "List View" key is in the main Title Bar next to the City Name.

To return to the "Icon" view and the main weather screen, simply perform a "Back" gesture on the Pre.

Using the "Tasks" App

The Pre comes with a very basic, yet very useful "Tasks" App that lets you keep track of important tasks. You can customize, add tasks and then "check them off" as they are accomplished. You can also organize tasks into groups.

Starting the Task App

Tap on the "Tasks" icon on your home screen. If you have already made tasks or "Synced" them from a program on your computer, they will be listed on the first screen. Just touch one of the tasks listed to see the sub menus and items to "check off."

Adding a new Task List

Touch the "Add Task" button

in the lower left hand corner. Give this Task a name. In this example, we are calling the task "Finish Book" and then listing the various things (sub-tasks) we need to do to get the book ready for publication.

Adding "To do" items in the Task Menu

Touch the "Add" icon in the lower left hand corner and type a name for the "To do" item inside this particular task.

In this example, we need to add three items; "Proof read," "Send to Martin" and "Send to Publisher."

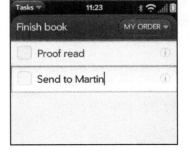

As I accomplish each task, I just touch the "check box" and put a check mark noting that the task is complete.

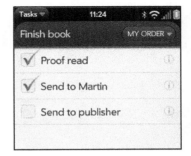

Chapter 24:
The App Catalog

We have just seen how easy it is download music, videos and right on your Pre. It is just as easy to download new applications from the Palm "App" Catalog. "Apps" are available initially in small numbers, since the "App Catalog" is still in "Beta," but we have been told that the number of "Apps" will increase greatly in the coming months.

Starting the App Catalog

The App catalog icon should be on your second page of icons on the Home Screen. Tap the icon to launch the "**App Catalog.**"

Along the top, there are "**Featured**" Apps. Below that are the "**Popular**" Apps.

Scroll down and you should see the "App" categories; "Most Recent," "Top Rated," "Lifestyle," "Entertainment," "Productivity," "Utilities," "News," "Social Networking," "Food," "Business," "Communications" and "Games."

Just touch any one of the categories and begin to scroll through the available Apps for download.

Finding an "App" to Download

Begin by looking around the default view – which is the **"Featured"** Apps and **"Popular"** Apps on the top. Swipe from right to left to see all the Apps in those two categories.

Change view to "Popular"

Like you did above, swipe the "Bar" of "Popular" Apps from right to left to see all the Apps in that category.

Using "Top Tags"

Sometimes, all the choices can be a bit overwhelming. If you have a sense of what type of App you are looking for, scroll down from where you see **"Top Tags"** to see all the available categories.

Find the Category of what you are searching for and touch the tab. So, if we knew we were looking for a "News" program, we would just touch the **"News"** category.

Scroll through the options until you find a "News" APP you want to download onto your Pre.

Searching for an App

Let's say you have a specific idea of what you are looking for. Touch the **"Search"** field and type in either the name of the program or the type of program.

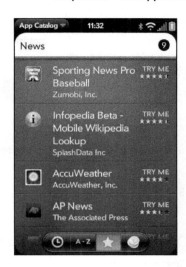

So, if you were looking for a News   program, just type in "News" and see what comes up. When you see something that resembles what you are searching for come up in the screen, just touch it.

Downloading Free or Paid Apps

Once you find the App you are looking for, you can download it right onto your Pre.

Locate the App you want to buy and notice the small button that either says

"Download"

"Try me." or Paid Apps will say "Download for a price" such as "Download for $4.99"

You might be prompted to "Allow" "Location Services" to be used for the application. Choose either "Continue" or "Don't Download" and proceed.

If you are sure that you want to purchase/install the App, just touch the "Continue" button.

Canceling the Download

If you decide that you wish to cancel the download, touch the "X" at the end of the status bar and the Download will be cancelled.

Finding Free or Discounted Apps

After browsing around you will notice a couple of things about the App catalog. First, there are lots of FREE apps. Sometimes these are great applications, other times, they are not so useful - but are fun!

The other thing that you will notice over time is that some of the apps will have sales, and some apps will become less expensive over time. So if you have a favorite app and it costs $6.99, it is likely that waiting a few weeks or a month might result in a lower price.

Updating your Apps

Quite often, developers will "update" their Apps for the Pre and Pre. You don't even need to use your Computer to perform the update –you can do it right on your Pre. There are a couple of ways "Updates" work on your Pre Apps.

The first way to check for updates is to go to the "Updates" icon on your Pre. Touch the "**Launcher**" arrow and swipe to the third screen.

Touch the "Updates" icon and the Pre will search for updates to your installed Apps and system software.

If it finds that updates are available, just touch the "**Update**" button and your App will be updated to the newest version.

The Second way to find "Updates" for Apps on the Pre is to touch the "**Most Recent**" tab under "**Top Tags**." If you see the name of an application already on your Pre with a small "star" in the corner – that means an update is available. Touch the application name and you will be prompted to "Update" the App.

Chapter 25: Fixing Problems

The Pre is a normally highly reliable. Occasionally, like your computer or any complicated electronic device, you might have to "reset" the device or troubleshoot a problem.

What to do if the Pre Stops Responding

Sometimes, your Pre won't respond to your touch – it freezes in the midst of the program. If this happens, the first thing to do is try to perform a "Back" gesture or "Swipe up" to minimize the program to a "Card."

If this doesn't work, try "tapping" the power button in the top right hand corner.

If this does not work – make sure you Pre isn't running out of power – try plugging it in or attaching it to your computer (if it's plugged in) and see if it will start to respond.

If the Pre continues to be unresponsive, try holding the "Power" button for about six or seven seconds – this should "quit" the program or give you the "shut down" option screen.

From this screen, you can choose to either "**Turn Off**" the Pre, go into "**Airplane**" mode (turn off the radio) or "**Cancel**" and try to continue using the device.

Sometimes, selecting the "Turn Off" option is a way of starting fresh. In this case, once the Pre powers down, you will need to hold the "Power" key for about three seconds and then let go – the Pre should power up in a few minutes.

Troubleshooting – Too many Cards

Sometimes, the Pre gets bogged down with too many open Apps or 'Cards.'

We have been able to have as many as 12 open cards at a time, but things do tend to slow down. Sometimes, even 4 or 5 might cause the Pre to drag.

In either case, the Pre will let you know when memory is running low with a "Sorry, Too Many Cards" error message like the one shown here.

In this situation, it is best to close all cards.

TIP: If your Pre is still running slowly, it might be good to try a simple "Reset" of the device to clear the memory. See the section below to learn how to Reset your Pre.

Resetting the Pre

Touch the "**Device Info**" icon

and scroll to the bottom of the screen. The last button at the bottom says "**Reset Options.**" Touch the "**Reset Options**" button.

The three options available are "**Restart,**" "**Partial Erase**" and "**Full Erase.**"

ALWAYS start with a "**Restart**" before you erase any information.

"**Partial Erase**" will erase all third party software you may installed data associated with those programs. Personal information, like Address book and Calendar entries will not be affected. Only choose this option if you think that a program you have installed is giving you trouble (like re-starting your phone.)

A "**Full Erase**" is something to use when you are perhaps going to the phone store to exchange your device and you want to remove all personal data.

NOTE: If the Pre is "too frozen" to open up the Device Info Screen (as shown above) you can press the "Orange Button" along with the "Sym" and "R" keys to reset the Pre.

 +  + = RESET

Running Built-In Tests on the Pre (Quick and Interactive)

In the Device Info Icon, bring up the menu and you will notice there are several tests you can run from the menu. There are "Quick Tests" and "Interactive Tests."

Quick Tests

These are a series of short tests that will test the hardware in the Pre to make sure it is all working correctly.

Select "Quick Tests" from the **Device Info** Icon menu and tap the "Start" button in the lower right corner.

To stop the tests, tap the "Stop" button.

If the tests all pass you will see a message on the screen. If some tests fail, then you will see the error codes and have a chance to send the results to customer service as shown to the right.

Interactive Tests

Select "**Interactive Tests**" from the **Device Info** Icon Menu to see all the options for various interactive tests.

Scroll down to see all the optional tests.

Tap any test to start it.

Dealing With Dropped Calls or Poor Service

While the Pre normally does a good job of "hanging on" to calls, occasionally, a call will be "dropped." Other times, you might be having trouble getting a signal –especially if you are "roaming."

There are a couple of settings you can occasionally "tweak" to minimize this.

Changing Settings from Phone Preferences

Start up the "**Phone**" App and the touch the "Carrier" tab in the top left hand corner. Select the "**Preferences**" tab and scroll to the bottom of the preferences screen.

Look at "Network Settings"

Touch the "**Voice Network**" setting and make sure this is set to "**Automatic**." Next, touch the "**Data Roaming**" tab and make sure this is set to "**Enabled**."

Update Network Settings

Touch the "**Update Network Settings**" tab and the Pre will go "Online" and make sure that all the latest cell phone towers are added to the "Network." This might improve your reception.

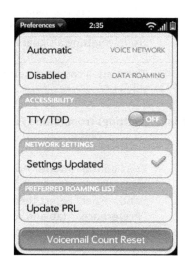

Update PRL

The "**Preferred Roaming Network**" is the network of "towers" which your carrier contracts with that may belong to other local networks to provide you with continual service if you are roaming or out of your local area.

These towers do change frequently, so occasionally "Updating the PRL" by just touching the "**Update PRL**" button can help you be connected wherever you go.

How to Reset the Pre

"Resetting" your Pre is your last response to an "unresponsive" Pre. It is perfectly safe, and usually fixes most problems.

The way to "Reset" your Pre is to use two hands and press and hold the "Power" button and while you do this, switch the "ringer" switch on and off about three times. You should then see the Palm® logo appear. When you see the logo, just release the buttons and your Pre will be reset.

Finally, you will need to power-on the Pre if it doesn't come on by itself.

Pre Does Not Show Up in iTunes

Occasionally, when you connect your Pres to your PC or Mac, your Pre may not recognized in the iTunes screen.

If this happens to you, the first thing to check is the battery charge of the Pre. If you have let the battery run too far down, iTunes won't see it until the level of the battery rises a bit.

If the battery is charged, try connecting the Pre to a different USB port on the computer. Sometimes, if you have always used one USB port for the Pre and switch it to another port, the computer won't see it.

If this still does not fix the problem try disconnecting the Pre and re-starting the computer. Then, reconnect the Pre to the USB port.

If this still does not work, it is possible that Palm and iTunes have once again become incompatible. If this happens, use the USB Drive mentioned on page 79 or another media manager like "doubleTwist" www.doubletwist.com or "Songbird" from www.songbird.org. (See our Media Transfer chapter for help 73.)

The latest version of iTunes can usually be found at: www.apple.com/itunes

No Sound in Music or Video

There are few things more frustrating than sitting down or moving about hoping to listen to music or watch a video and no sound comes out of the Pre. Usually, there is an easy fix for this problem.

The first thing to do may seem obvious, but unplug your headphones (if you are using them) and then put them back in. Sometimes, the headset jack just isn't connected well.

If that doesn't fix the problem – check the volume. You might have accidentally lowered the volume all the way.

Next, make sure the song or video is not in "Pause" mode. Bring up the   music or video controls   Once you bring up the controls, verify the song is not PAUSED or the volume is not turned down all the way.

Next, check the "**Volume**" to see if you (or someone else) have turned the "Volume" of the phone all the way down.

Make sure that your Pre is not connected to a Bluetooth device. Sometimes, your Pre might "connect" to a paired Bluetooth headset or stereo and the music our sounds might be playing through that Bluetooth device instead of the speakers.

Touch the "**Bluetooth**" icon at the top of the Pre and touch the "**Bluetooth**" tab. Scroll through your Bluetooth devices and see if you are accidentally connected. If you are, just touch the tab and disconnect or turn off Bluetooth altogether – just look at page 124 for more information.

If none of these options help, bring your Pre back to the place of purchase for repair.

Restoring you Pre from a Backup

Sometimes, you might have to "restore" your Pre to an earlier or even its original state. Usually, you would only do this is you did a "Full Erase" as you did above, or if you had to return your Pre for a new device.

Backup is Automatic

Backup on the Pre is truly simple – you don't have to think about it.

Once you create your "Palm Profile" as you did on page 54, your device will periodically Backup itself without you initiating anything.

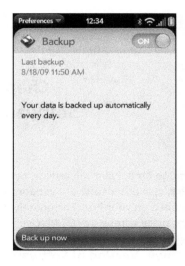

Restore from Previous Backup

If you perform a "Full Erase" as you did above, or if you have to "swap out" your device for a new one, you will be asked to input your palm profile information. Just put in the email address and password you selected when you created the Palm Profile.

You will receive a warning (if this is a new device) that another device has that profile setting – and then all your Apps and information will be "Pulled" from their various hosts and put into the new device.

NOTE: Things like "Ringtones," "Volume" and "Brightness" settings and perhaps some "linked contacts"   may not fully restore.

Chapter 26:
Software Updates

From time to time, Palm will release new versions of the system software that runs on the Pre, also other software vendors will release updates for the new icons you have installed on your Pre. Fortunately, updating your Pre software is something that takes place wirelessly "OTA" (Over –The – Air) and is very easy to do.

When a new Version of Software is Released

Palm will usually notify you with an alert on the screen whenever a new version of the webOS™ system software is released. As we were completing this book, Palm has recently rolled out version 1.2 of the system software. You can expect new features will continue to be introduced as webOS™ evolves.

From time-to-time, you should check the Updates icon for any updates of software you have installed on your Pre, from the App Catalog or from other locations.

Using the "Updates" App

On your Launcher icon screens (usually on the third screen) is an icon that looks like a small box and says "**Updates**."

Touch the "**Updates**" icon and the Pre will check for available updates – for both the system software (webOS™) and for any application icons you might have installed.

If you receive a notice informing you that there is a "Software Update," we recommend that you choose to update either the application or the System software at that time.

Updating the OS

If there is a webOS™ system software update, the Pre will immediately begin to download the update. The download progress will be shown in the status bar at the bottom.

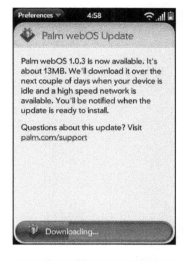

You will see the size of the update – the image at the right shows 13MB and that the device will download it slowly over time – so it does not disrupt your work.

Once the update is complete, the notification screen will prompt you to "**Install**" the update. Touch the "**Install Now**" button at the bottom of the screen.

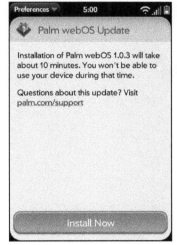

TIP: Most system software updates will take about 10 minutes and you cannot use your device during that time – so pick a time when you won't mind not having access to your device. (Very late night or very early morning might be the best.)

The Update screen will go through a "**Validation**" process and then you will see an "**Update Installed**" screen letting you know that the update was complete.

Touch "**Done**" and your Pre is now updated and ready to use.

Chapter 27:
Video Tutorials & More

Made Simple Learning Short Video Training
Perfect for You and Your Entire Organization

By the time you read this, we should have a number of short 3-minute video tutorials for the Palm® Pre™. We also add new videos from our customer feedback, so email us at info@madesimplelearning.com with any suggestion for new videos to add to the growing library.

ONLINE ACCESS TO VIDEOS: WWW.MADESIMPLELEARNING.COM
You may purchase access for yourself online at our web site: www.madesimplelearning.com. This will give you an extended time to access the video tutorials (1 year) and electronic book. Enterprise licensing is also available.

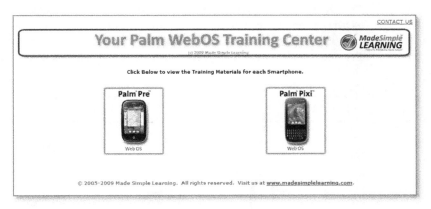

OFFLINE ACCESS TO VIDEOS: TRAINING CENTER DVD-ROM

If you prefer to load up everything on your computer, and skip having to go online, then we offer you the option of purchasing the entire Training Center (Videos for your computer, Palm Pre and e-Book for your computer) on a DVD-ROM.

The choice is yours: Whether you purchase the ONLINE access or DVD-ROM version, you can watch the 3-minute "*Videos Now*" on your computer (PC or Mac), watch the 3-minute "*Videos To Go*" on your Palm Pre and read the *Made Simple* electronic Book (electronic version of this book) on your computer.

Use our keyword search feature to pinpoint exactly the video you need, exactly when you need it.

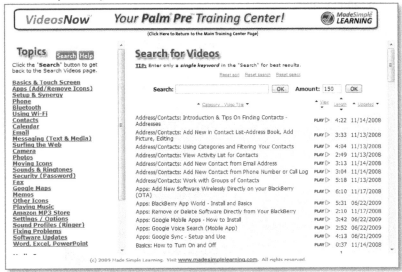

(NOTE: Topics and videos listed will change somewhat – above is for illustrative purposes only.)

You can also click any topic in the left column to browse the videos by topic.

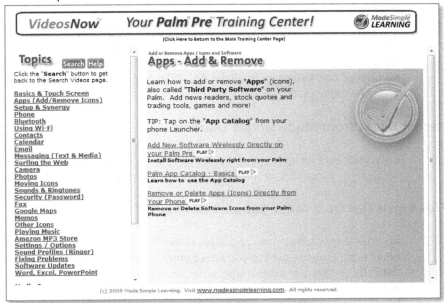

(NOTE: Topics and videos listed will change somewhat – above is for illustrative purposes only.)

We keep our videos short and to-the-point – most average just 3 minutes in running time.

Gone are the days of trying to puzzle out how to do something. You can just watch and learn by seeing the expert do it on their Palm Pre.

We listen to our customers and watch development with new Palm webOS™ operating system versions and models to add new videos frequently. When you check out the site, it's quite likely there will be a number of new videos on the Palm Pre, Palm Pixi, BlackBerry Smartphones and other devices.

Recent Books from Made Simple Learning

Keep your eyes on www.madesimplelearning.com and on www.amazon.com for all the new books and Training Centers DVD-ROMs.

Free Email Tips from Made Simple Learning

Another way to learn more about your Palm Pre is to sign up for our short email tips. They are sent to you about twice a week. These tips are great 'bite-size' nuggets of useful information to help you get the most out of your Pre. Sign up anytime for free tips at www.MadeSimpleLearning.com, look for the webOS™ (Pre/Pixi) free tips.

Help on the Device

If you have a question about how something works and you cannot find an answer in this book or from the video tutorials, a good place to start is the "Help" item found on most of the menus.

Help on the Palm Pre provides mostly text-based help files, however, there are a few silent animations that can be useful.

Where to go for more information?

Many Palm Pre owners would be classified as "Enthusiasts" and are part of any number of Palm Pre user groups and online discussion forums. These user groups along with various forums and web sites serve as a great resource for Palm Pre users.

Forums and Discussion Groups such as "PreCentral" and "BlackBerry Forums." A forum is an organized discussion about anything and everything BlackBerry. On each of these sites, you can discuss your BlackBerry, find tips and tricks as well as post questions and read answers to other user's questions.

At time of publishing, here are a few of these more popular forums.
www.precentral.net
www.everyghingpre.com
www.palmpreforum.com
www.palmprehacks.net

And, of course the official palm discussion forum:
forums.palm.com

Online Forum Etiquette

Step 1: SEARCH FIRST
Perform a thorough search of what is on the site in the forums before you post a new question. More than 50% of the time, the question you asked has already been asked and answered. Nothing will get you a sharp rebuke faster than posting a question that has already been answered several times elsewhere in the forums or FAQ sections.

Step 2: POST IN THE CORRECT AREA

If you have searched and cannot find the question you need answered, browse the forum topics and try to pick the one that works best for your question.

Step 3: BE AS SPECIFIC AS POSSIBLE

When writing your question, give as much detail as possible to help people to respond correctly.

POORLY WORDED (TOO LITTLE DETAIL): "Email stopped working on my Pre"

GOOD DETAIL IN QUESTION: "When I try to send a message from my Pre, I see an error message that says 'unable to send – network error 1235"

Palm Developer Site – Developing Your Own webOS™ Apps

If you are interested in trying your hand at developing applications for the Palm Pre to submit to the App Catalog, please check out http://developer.palm.com/. This is the official web site to get started with webOS™ app development for the Palm Pre, Pixi and future webOS™ devices.

From this site you can download the Palm Mojo Software Development Kit (SDK) and obtain access to lots of great training tools to learn how to use the tools to build your first app.

Thanks Again!

Again, we sincerely thank you for purchasing this book and hope it has helped you really learn how to get every last drop of productivity and fun out of your Palm Pre™!

Chapter 28:
Homebrew Apps

(This Chapter was written by **Dieter Bohn**, Editor in Chief of SmartPhone Experts. Dieter runs the popular Palm Pre webOS™ blog at www.PreCentral.net)

In addition to the official apps that are available on Palm's own App Catalog, there is a thriving community of developers and 'power users' who are creating and using unofficial applications also called 'homebrew' applications.

A homebrew app is simply an app you install on your Pre without using Palm's App Catalog. You should know that installing homebrew apps isn't as easy as installing official ones. Almost all homebrew apps are also 'Beta,' which means that some may have bugs in them. You should only install homebrew apps if you feel comfortable with that.

Where to Find Homebrew Apps

There are several sites that offer homebrew apps, most notably PreCentral.net. The homebrew apps you can find there range from simple games to highly sophisticated podcast managers. In fact, more than a dozen of these apps have 'graduated' into the official Palm App Catalog. You can find a gallery of homebrew apps here:

http://www.precentral.net/homebrew-apps

How to Setup your Pre to Accept Homebrew Apps

There is a detailed set of instructions on how to get started with homebrew apps here:

http://www.precentral.net/how-to-install-homebrew-apps

Briefly, though, the basic method for getting your Pre set up for homebrew involves just a few steps.

1. Turn on 'Developer Mode.' This makes your Pre 'rooted' and 'open' to any computer that you plug it into via USB. You can turn on developer mode by typing 'webos20090606' (no quotes) in the launcher screen. This will reveal the Developer Mode icon, which you can tap. Your Pre will reset.

2. Download 'webOS™ Quick Install.' This application that you download and install on your desktop is how you will install your first homebrew app. You can find it here

http://forums.precentral.net/homebrew-apps/206905-webos-quick-install-v2-7-beyond.html

The first time you run webOS™ Quick Install, it will download a large file from Palm's website and then need to be re-launched. Let it do that, following the on-screen prompts on your desktop.

3. Plug your Pre in and tap 'Just Charge' and then launch webOS™ Quick Install on your desktop.

4. Within webOS™ Quick Install, you can click on the icon with a green arrow on it. That will open up a screen that can download homebrew apps directly from the web. On the window that pops up, check the box next to 'fileCoaster,' click 'Download,' and then click 'close.' Now click the 'Install!' button to install the app!

5. Now you may unplug your Pre. I recommend you repeat step 1, above, to turn OFF Developer Mode. If you leave your Pre in Developer Mode, it can be a security risk.

6. You can now use the fileCoaster app to browse and install homebrew applications directly on your Pre.

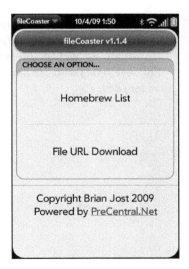

Homebrew 'Patches'

In addition to homebrew apps, even more advanced users and developers are installing homebrew 'patches,' which alter the core files of the Palm Pre to do clever things like change the Pre's theme, alter how the calendar works, and so on.

You can find out more information on how to work with homebrew patches and tweaks by visiting either PreCentral.net or http://webos-internals.org. webOS-internals is an open source, international community of developers who are discovering new things that the Pre is capable of every day.

INDEX

INDEX

Made Simple Learning, 14
Free Email Tips, 338
Recent Books, 338
Videos To Go(tm), 14
Made Simple Learning
Video Training, 335
Maps
Add Information to Contacts, 293
Change the Mape View, 289
Checking Traffic, 290
Choose Start or End Location, 294
Determine Your Location, 288
Direction List, 296
Getting Directions, 294
Getting Started with Google
Maps, 288
Looking at Route, 295
Search for Anything, 291
Using the GPS, 296
Viewing Options, 289
Zooming in and Out, 294
Media
Overview, 17
Media Player
Overview, 17
Media Transfer
Sync to PC, 96
Media Transfer
Create iTunes Playlist, 86
Download iTunes, 84
iTunes Basics, 85
iTunes Sign In, 91
Loading CDs into iTunes, 92
Running iTunes for first time, 84
Set uo Media Sync on Pre, 88
Media Transfer
Get Album Artwork, 97
Media Transfer Manually Put Music
on Pre, 93
MemoPad
Overview, 17
Memos
Add new Memo, 298
Changing Color of, 302
Deleting, 301
Editing, 300
Emailing, 301
Getting Started, 297

Sorting, 298
Viewing and Editing, 299
Messaging
Reply to SMS, 199
Send Photo via MMS, 203
SMS from contacts, 198
SMS Notification Options, 200
View Stored Messages, 200
Music
Adjusting Volume, 259
Albums view, 255
Artists View, 254
iPod Icon, 253
Play Previous or Next Song, 258
Playing Music, 257
Playlist View, 256
Repeat and Shuffle, 260
Searching for Music, 254
Shuffle Icon, 261
Songs View, 255
Notes
Overview, 17
Pandora
Bookmark or Purchase Song, 285
Build Stations, 283
Change Preferences, 287
Download App, 283
Listening to, 284
See all Stations, 286
Set up Account, 282
Starting, 282
Photos
Assign Picture to Contact, 239
Choose Photo Library, 235
Deleting Picture, 240
Double Tapping, 237
Emailing Picture, 239
Launch Photos Icon, 234
Moving Between Pictures, 236
Pinching, 238
Send as MMS, 241
Using as Wallpaper, 238
View Pictures, 235
Zooming In and Out, 237
Products
Other Books, 14
Videos viewed on BlackBerry, 14
Quick Launch Bar, 39
Moving Icons to, 242

Free Tips and Video Tutorials online at www.MadeSimpleLearning.com   **347**

www.ingramcontent.com/pod-product-compliance
Lightning Source LLC
Chambersburg PA
CBHW071403050326
40689CB00010B/1743